ENDORSEMENTS

"Serge Gasore miraculously lived through the genocide in Rwanda, but not without witnessing unthinkable horrors and the slaughter of his closest relatives. This account of what he saw and how he survived will break your heart, but his faith and spirit and willingness to forgive will inspire you. 'My Day to Die' is an unbelievable story, except that it is true."

Tom Gjelten
Author, <u>Sarajevo Daily: A City and Its Newspaper Under Siege</u>

"I first knew Serge Gasore while watching him run as an exceptional athlete on the Abilene Christian University cross-country team. Soon our conversations were about his country, Rwanda. Over the years the conversations grew deeper and more personal as I discovered Serge Gasore as a remarkable young man with a truly inspiring story. I'm pleased he has agreed to share his story in this book —as you read it you will understand why I'm thankful I know Serge Gasore."

Gary McCaleb
Vice President, Abilene Christian University
Mayor of Abilene, Texas (1990-1999)

"This inspirational book by Serge Gasore is a 'MUST READ' especially for people of faith, throughout the world! His dramatic story will leave a lasting impression with every reader who is fortunate enough to obtain a copy of it."

Dr. Robert D. (Bob) Hunter
Senior Vice President Emeritus
Abilene Christian University
Texas State Representative 1987-2007

"Serge's story is stunning and grabs your heart from the first page to the last. It is almost impossible to imagine his description of the evil and devastation of the Rwandan genocide but at the same time, he shares the amazing grace that comes from Serge's faith through surrender. He reminds us that we are all sons and daughters of God and His desire is for us to forgive even the 'unforgiveable' as we have been forgiven. This incredible story will richly bless you and can't help but change your life."

Robin Blakeley
President, Pursuant Sports

MY DAY TO DIE

TO DIE

RUNNING FOR MY LIFE

SERGE GASORE

with Patsy Watson

ARCHWAY
PUBLISHING

Archway Publishing books may be ordered through booksellers or by contacting:

Archway Publishing
1663 Liberty Drive
Bloomington, IN 47403
www.archwaypublishing.com
1-(888)-242-5904

Because of the dynamic nature of the Internet, any web addresses or
links contained in this book may have changed since publication and
may no longer be valid. The views expressed in this work are solely those
of the author and do not necessarily reflect the views of the publisher,
and the publisher hereby disclaims any responsibility for them.

Any people depicted in stock imagery provided by Thinkstock are models,
and such images are being used for illustrative purposes only.
Certain stock imagery © Thinkstock.

ISBN: 978-1-4808-0581-1 (sc)
ISBN: 978-1-4808-0582-8 (e)

Library of Congress Control Number: 2014903056

Printed in the United States of America

Archway Publishing rev. date: 02/26/2014

FOREWORD

Christmas break was beginning at Abilene Christian University, and a graduate student by the name of Ryan Campbell gave me a call. Ryan was leaving town for several days, and he was calling to ask if my family and I would host his roommate, an international student from Rwanda, for a meal sometime over the break. Ryan told me his roommate's name was Serge Gasore.

I agreed to contact Serge and invite him to our home, and that is the short version of how I was blessed by God with a son. Serge joined Susan, Katie Lea, Caroline and me for Christmas dinner, and we all seemed to know we'd found a new brother and son.

Since that day several years ago, Serge has grown to be even more a part of my heart and life. Over many conversations he revealed the story of his early years in Rwanda, his ordeal within the horror of the genocide, and his life being miraculously spared on multiple occasions. Serge has spoken to me of his coming to the United States with a broken faith, and how our gracious and loving Father restored the broken pieces of his faith to wholeness. I had the privilege of officiating at the wedding ceremony when Serge took Esperance to be his wife. I now have two grandsons, Serge Jr. and Joel, both of who bear a slight resemblance to me. (That's my story and I'm sticking to it.)

During the summer of 2013, Susan and I, along with our dear friend, Karen Vaughn, had the incredible opportunity to spend nearly two weeks in Rwanda alongside Serge. That life-changing trip allowed me to step into the experiences Serge had described to me over the years. I strolled through his village, Ntarama. I walked upon the patch of land upon which had stood Serge's grandmother's house prior to the genocide. I touched the hole the grenade blast had created in the wall of the small church building in Ntarama, the hole through which Serge had fled the vicious mob surrounding the church building intent on killing all inside. In short, I retraced the path Serge ran as a young boy out of Rwanda and witnessed full circle Serge as the man God is calling back to Rwanda.

During my time in Rwanda I had the privilege of witnessing firsthand Serge's passion for the people of his country, his deep sense of mission and calling by God, and his incredible love for children. Serge is a gifted-by-God leader. I jokingly called Serge "Moses" on several occasions during our time in Rwanda, but the many parallels between Moses' and Serge's lives are striking.

Serge was rescued from almost certain death as a child. He grew to be a strong young man, an athlete — a swift runner. Serge was provided the opportunity to journey to a land with great material and educational resources, and achieved a position based on accomplishment and education that would cause many in his country to view him as a "prince." Yet Serge has never forgotten his people.

Serge feels a burning desire from God in his heart and soul to return to Rwanda, to be a leader among his people, to be an advocate for education as the best resource to free the minds of his people from poverty and oppression, to be God's instrument in rescuing children, much as he was rescued by God when the shadow of death was near, and to be a bright light for Jesus of peace, hope, forgiveness and love.

This book is about Serge's story, but even more, it is the story of God's incredible grace and mercy.

Vann Conwell
January 2014

ACKNOWLEDGEMENTS

God be glorified for giving me life up to this day and for my most beautiful wife, Esperance Gasore, and my handsome sons, Serge Gasore, Junior and Joel Vann Gasore.

Special thanks go to my best friend and wife, Esperance, who supports me in everything. I would not be who I am today if I did not have a loving and caring wife.

Special thanks also go to Lorin and Patsy Watson, who made everything about this book possible, and who have been very good friends of our family since I got to America. The memory of driving with you out in the country for more than 30 miles to get the American Christmas tree lives in my mind. In particular, I want to thank Patsy for the hours she spent with me, listening to my story and capturing the words on paper.

I want to say thanks to Kevin and Victoria Watson Johnson for their friendship that goes beyond. The time we spend together enjoying snow cones brings joy in me. I also want extend a special thanks to Victoria Watson Johnson for taking time to read and edit my story.

Thanks to all my family and extended family – those in Rwanda as well as in the United States of America. In Rwanda, thanks to my uncle, Antoine Sebera Nyunga, and his wife, Muzana Alice, for the encouraging messages they sent my way every single day while I was writing this book.

Special thanks to Vann and Susan Conwell, my adoptive parents, and their two daughters, Caroline and Katie Lea, for everything they did in order for this book to be written, and especially to Katie Lea for designing the cover of my book.

Also, thanks, too, to Shane and Melissa McClung for their contribution toward this book.

This book is dedicated to the many children who are facing wars, abuse, neglect, oppression and poverty around the world. I stay awake many times thinking of many innocent children who are being killed in Congo, Sudan, Somalia, Mexico, Iraq, Afghanistan, Iraq and Syria, and many other developing countries like Haiti and Mexico where children are victims of poverty or societal violence. I have been through situations like this - for example when I went through the genocide and even after the genocide. I have had to deal with the consequences such as poverty, abuse, neglect, oppression and family violence. My friends were dying in front of me and the whole world closed its eyes at that time, and now it looks like the same things are happening to many children of Syria and Sudan. I dare leaders of this world to stop being selfish and ignorant. These kids need their help.

CONTENTS

PREFACE

I first met Serge Gasore in 2006, at an NCAA track meet in Emporia, Kan. It was not until a few years later that I got to know more about him and his incredible story.

Serge and several other college students were sitting around our table one Sunday, eating together. The discussion had somehow turned to our daughter's phobia of snakes. During this discussion, Serge very quietly stated, "When it was my day to die, there were snakes in the tree I was tied to."

Serge quietly continued the conversation regarding snakes, but I could not shake his comment from my mind, and asked him to tell me what he meant by "my day to die."

Serge then told those of us gathered there that day an almost unbelievable story of tragedy and triumph, which will be shared with you in this book.

Never have I known anyone with more reason to hate and be bitter, and yet never have I known a more kind, gentle, loving and forgiving person.

Serge's story is sure to horrify you and bless you, as it has me. He was only four years old when his mother was brutally murdered almost in front of his eyes. At the young age of seven, he was pulled into the middle of the terrible genocide of Rwanda. Following the genocide, Serge served in the Rwandan Patriotic Front as a boy solider. This is his story – a story of a young boy who somehow found survival – and then peace. Blessings to all who read it.

Patsy Watson

INTRODUCTION

Everyone on the earth has a story and in each story there are struggles and barriers. People should always keep in mind that everyone is fighting battles and is trying to overcome them. Our prayers must always go out to them. In this book, I will be sharing my life story. I have found it helpful to share my life story because it helps me to remove my stress. Also, I am convinced that it can be a way of changing the world.

I will summarize my life story, specifically trying to identify people, events, spiritual struggles, spiritual victories past and things that have been involved in my spiritual journey.

Many times during my early life, I did not know if I would be alive the next day. But I can remember that God put words in me. He told me, "You are alive for a reason. Don't give up. Just keep pushing. If you live, it is good. If you die, it is okay."

-Serge Gasore

RWANDA – A BRIEF OVERVIEW

To understand my story, you must have some understanding of my history. To look to the future, we must have a solid understanding of the past. I will tell you briefly about Rwanda, my home.

Rwanda is a small country located in the central east part of Africa. Rwanda's population is 11,457,801 people, and the country covers an area of 10,169 square miles, which is smaller than the state of Maryland. While there is no denying the atrocity of Rwanda's past, the country is seeking to build a brighter future.

Three main cultural groups exist in Rwanda – the Hutu, Tutsi and Twa. The Hutu are traditionally associated with land, the Tutsi with cows and the Twa with forest. Historically, affiliation with a group was determined by your father's ancestry and intermarriage was common.

Prior to the genocide, my country was divided into three tribes, the Abahutu (Hutu), the Abatutsi (Tutsi) and the Abatwa (Twa).

The Hutu were the majority tribe. They were in power since 1959. From the president to the bottom of the political structure, probably 99 percent of the government was Hutu. The Hutu were identified by early German and Belgium colonists as being shorter and stout in stature, and having big noses. Hutu were very strong physically. They were normally business people and, because the majority of the government was Hutu, were well supported in everything they did. The Hutu who lived in the cities were teachers, lawyers or other professionals because they were picked out for higher education. However, the Hutu who lived in the villages were farmers and had very little. They did not have as many cows as the Tutsi. The Hutu were not ranchers, so they bought their milk from Tutsi.

The Tutsi, as identified by the colonists, were tall and thin, with thinner noses. Physically, they did not look as strong as the Hutu. The Tutsi were the minority. They were ranchers and raised a lot of cattle. People said the Tutsi were very smart. They did not get as much opportunity to go to school, but those who attended school were very smart. In 1959, the Hutu government moved most of the Tutsi to the central part of Rwanda, and some to the south, which meant Tutsi were found in the same areas, so a lot of times Tutsi were living in the same cities.

The Twa were people considered to be pygmies because of their size, as well as their language and behavior. They were a minority and lived off making pottery from mud. The Twa also used the mud to make bricks. Most of them lived by rivers or in valleys, where they would have access to the specific mud needed to make the pottery. The pottery was not very substantial. The Twa did not sell the pottery for money, but traded it for food or clothes. They were not looking for money to get rich or to go to school or anything. Because they did not attend school, the Twa were not well-educated. The Hutu government used the Twa to persecute people the government opposed. The Twa were easy to use because any little thing made them happy and made them do something for you.

I remember one time I was on the street, eating a corn on the cob, and some Twa passed by with pottery on their head. I think they were going to sell them, but when they saw me eating the corn, they asked me, "Can you share with us?" Being young and very stupid and stubborn, I said, "no." They cursed me and said, "Keep it and may it bury you when you die." This was a common curse in our country and an example of why I believe the Twa had very common behavior, or bad manners.

The Twa played a very minor role in the genocide, but I cannot blame them because they had no education. The Twa had no problem with the Tutsi, but were paid to do what they did and were told that if they killed you they could take whatever you had, so it was easy for them to take your stuff.

I remember a very sad story. When we were camping at my school during the genocide, three people from the Twa tribe came to our camp. Before they got to where we were hiding, the Twa ran to the house of a very rich person and found food on the stove (a wood-burning cook stove). They smelled the food and instead of coming after us, the Twa jumped the fence to the house where the food was. As they were jumping, some of the people in our camp saw them and realized they were Twa coming after us. Immediately our people called the crowd and said, "We saw Twa going to this house, and let's go after them." So all the guys in our camp went after the Twa and killed them in a very bad way. The guys in our camp were very angry they were being hunted after having just survived, so they took out their anger on the Twa who were coming to kill them, and treated the Twa badly. I remember the bodies of the Twa lay there a long time, and I will never forget that image. I remember, when I was running away, passing by those bodies and the smell of death.

During the genocide, you could even hear the Twa coming because their language was different. If the Twa found you, you knew that was all. Right now, the government is trying to teach the Twa and the Twa now have representatives in our Congress, where before there was no Twa representation. The Twa have young representatives who campaign for their rights and they are being educated, so their future is more positive and changing for the better. Because the Twa are not mentioned a lot in discussions of my country, it makes it seem as though there are only two tribes in Rwanda and this is why the Tutsi are considered the minority.

The Tutsi who wanted to get an education many times had to go to neighboring countries. My Dad and my uncle, who went to Congo to get an education, are examples of this. They knew that if they attended school in Rwanda they would never pass because the Hutu professors would make sure they stayed behind by giving them lower grades. The Tutsi who were able to receive an education in Rwanda were mistreated. In order to receive a scholarship, the Tutsi's grades had to be higher than the Hutu's, so there wasn't much possibility of the Tutsi getting scholarships.

All of the tribes of Rwanda speak Kinyarwanda. However, the language of the people who live in the north part of the country is a little bit different. The majority of these people are Hutu. The Twa speak a very broken Kinyarwanda because they were apart from the rest of society, so they ended up forming their own language. As in most countries, people from different parts of the country speak with different accents.

The Hutu and Tutsi have a unique relationship that took center stage in Rwanda's history. The Hutu and Tutsi relationship is defined by a system known as *ubuhake,* which is a system where Hutus would go and work for Tutsi, and in return they would be given livestock, temporary pastures, and food. From the 1400s until the 1960s Rwanda existed as a monarchy, ruled by a lineage of Tutsi kings and a hierarchy of Tutsi noble and gentry. Overall, this monarchy served as a unifying symbol for Rwanda, representing the interest of Tutsi, Hutu and Twa ethnic groups and allowing the population to live together without divisions among them. However, this harmony was eventually disrupted by colonization.

Rwanda was first colonized by Germany in 1899. In 1919, after World War I, control was passed to Belgium. The colonial rulers developed policies that encouraged greater ethnic identification, which favored the Tutsi at the expense of the Hutu. They developed a centralized political system and introduced ideas of nationalism. The monarchy and *ubuhake* were seen as systems by which the Hutu exploited the Tutsi.

Tensions increased when Rwanda gained independence from Belgium in 1962. The Tutsi king was deposed by Hutu politicians in 1969, which furthered tension among

Rwandans. With a Hutu government in power, over the next few decades violence against the Tutsi increased. Many Tutsi fled or were driven out of Rwanda and into neighboring countries. In 1990, Tutsi exiles formed the Rwandan Patriotic Front (RPF) in Uganda. They started a civil war in Rwanda, which, combined with political and economic problems and worsening ethnic tensions, culminated in the 1994 state-led genocide. During this time, Rwandans killed up to a million of their fellow citizens and approximately three-quarters of the Tutsi population.

Later in 1994, the RPF ousted the government, ending the violence. Rwanda now has a policy of nondiscrimination, which allowed the country to make great gains in reconstruction and reconciliation since 1994. This policy allowed social change for the country's betterment. Rwanda now has an established government, which is stable, and the country instituted a new constitution, which implemented the separation of three branches of power, the Legislative, Executive and Judicial. The government is fighting corruption within and creating an effective justice system. Decentralization is one of the tools the government uses to lead the country. This policy made a big difference by giving more power to the local leaders. This policy is effective because these leaders are closer to the people and it is easier for them to transform the citizens' lives.

In recent years, especially, Rwanda made substantial "socio-economic and political progress" and furthered the era of peace, stability and social cohesion among Rwandans.[1]

---

1   United States. Congress. Congressional Research Service. *Rwanda: Background and Current Developments*. By Ted Dagne. Congressional Research Service, 1 June 2011. Web. May 2012.

The genocide was a systematic destruction of the Tutsi tribe. The genocide can be described as being much like what happens when one prepares one's house to be rid of unwanted insects. First, you prepare all your kitchen cabinets by taking out the things you do not want to be contaminated by the spray and moving them to a safe place. Then, you spray and spray with the pesticide, making sure you spray every shelf in the cabinet and every corner of the shelf. You move shelf by shelf until you have covered the entire kitchen. While you are doing this, you inform your friends and neighbors of what you are doing, so that they stay away from your house. Also, before you spray you train those who will be doing the spraying, so they can make sure that all the insects are gone.

This is the way the Hutu were able to destroy the Tutsi. The Hutu went into every province of the country, house by house, so the Tutsi were not safe no matter where they went. In fact, the Tutsi were referred to as "cockroaches."

EARLY LIFE – BEFORE THE GENOCIDE

The land we lived on is in the part of Rwanda called *Bugesera*. To a native of Rwanda, this brings to mind a flat, dry place. The climate has two main seasons – dry season and rainy season. The dry season lasts from the end of May until the end of September. From October through February, the temperatures are very moderate, and rain falls occasionally. Rainy season lasts from the beginning of March to the end of April, with warm temperatures, which range from 70 to 90 degrees during the day and drop into the 60s at night. Mountain areas of the country have colder temperatures, which drop into the 40s at night. The mountainous areas are much more humid, with a heavy mist that hangs in the air during the rainy season.

During the time of the kingdom in Rwanda, the king divided the country into what you might call "zones" and chose leaders, known as chiefs, to be in charge of each zone. A zone was the equivalent of what is called a county in the United States.

A chief would resolve conflicts and lead the people of his area. He served in the king's palace for a set period of time. Each chief had servants to tend to his needs and care for his land, his crops and his cattle. Because of his power, people would often come to the chief to offer him bribes or gifts, such as land, cows, etc.

My grandfather was chosen to be a chief because of his reputation as a wise and respected man. Grandfather was also known for his hospitality and generosity. One story I heard about him was how he made banana beer and invited everyone to come share.

At the time of the kingdom, the Hutu were slaves to the Tutsi. Because my grandfather was a kind man, his servants were very loyal to him. When the Hutu overthrew the king, my grandfather lost most of his land and what he owned. My grandfather had many followers go with him as refugees to a different part of the country. Many of these followers were Hutu who were his servants.

My grandfather had twelve children, including my father. Three of his children were killed in the genocide, as was his wife. Eight of his children still live in Rwanda. My grandfather wanted his children to get an education. Two of his sons, including my father, went to school in Congo because they could get a better education there. After the overthrow of the king, the Tutsi were heavily discriminated against in Rwanda, and this was true in the schools as well. Seeing that his children were educated paid off for my grandfather because, as a result of their education, his children were able to build a house for him and my grandmother.

Even though Grandfather died before I was born, I heard many stories about him and his kindness. He was well-known and his name is still recognized in Rwanda today.

I was born in Gashora, Rwanda in 1986 – a peaceful time in Rwanda. Immediately after I was born, we moved to Kigali, which is the capital city of Rwanda. We lived there for about a year and then moved to Ntarama.

My father is a Tutsi named Augustin Nyunga, and my mother was a Tutsi named Mujawamariya Beate. I am an only child.

Life was good and revolved around family, friends and neighbors. We all shared with each other. When we cooked food, we called out to our neighbors and they came to our home and ate with us. It was this closeness and sharing that made what happened later so hard to understand.

In 1994, my country was ravaged by genocide. "**Genocide** is the deliberate and systematic destruction, in whole or in part, of an ethnic, racial, religious, or national group."[2] I remember happy times before the genocide. A typical day might find me at my grandmother's house, playing without a care. As long as I can remember, I lived with my grandmother. My dad had moved to Kigali to find work because there was no work in the village where we lived. He found employment with the Office of the Treasury, and still has a position with them even now. My mom also worked in the city, and I stayed with my grandmother. Mom came on holidays to visit and check on me. I remember that my mom really cared a lot about me. There were no phones, so the only way to communicate was by sending messages back and

2   "Genocide." *Wikipedia*. Wikimedia Foundation, 17 Jan. 2014. Web. 18 May 2012. ["Important note: The Wikimedia Foundation does not own copyright on Wikipedia article texts and illustrations." Copied from Wikipedia website, January 20, 2014.]

forth with someone who came from the capital city. My mother would ask my grandmother, "Is he doing okay?" "He's not sick, is he?"

My dad sent money to my grandmother through a rich man who lived nearby. This man was very well-known and had a business delivering stones and bricks to the village, so Dad sent money, messages and medicine for me to my grandmother through him. I did not get to see my dad very often, maybe just twice a year. For this reason, we were not especially close. During the genocide, my dad had an employee who was a Hutu, who protected him from the killers. My dad hid on the roof of a house and survived during this time. After the genocide, when I was going to high school, my dad and I reconnected and he became a part of my life and helped me in so many ways. My daddy's sisters lived in other provinces of the country, and on their way to visit Grandmother, they stopped by to see my dad and brought messages to my grandmother.

When I was little, I had a big, big memory. Sometimes, maybe, I wish it wasn't quite so big. The day my mother died still haunts me. I was only four years old. She was working in the garden outside my grandmother's house and I was on the front porch. I heard a horrible noise – and I called my grandmother, who was inside. My grandmother immediately said, "Let's go see what happened." As we ran into the garden, we saw my mother lying there. We screamed and our neighbors came. I remember after that we called my father. He came down for her burial. A lot of family and friends came. We gathered and we buried my mother. After that, my grandmother decided that I would officially stay with her. My grandmother treated me as a son. She treated me well and she was always very kind to me. She showed a lot of emotion to me that showed she cared for me, but when the genocide began in 1994 she was killed.

After my mother's death, I was too young to think about the future, and because I was used to living with my grandmother, I did not worry about having someone to take care of me. Because I lived with my grandmother, I knew that she would continue to take care of me and keep treating me well. My aunt Agnes, on my father's side, lived nearby, and she helped me go through the grieving process, because she was my grandmother's right hand. Any time I was sick, and my grandmother was sick at the same time, my aunt made food and checked on us. My uncle Eugene, who was also my grandmother's right hand, was also very close to us and any time anything went wrong he came over. The loss of my mother did not stay in my mind until after the genocide when I had also lost my grandmother. This is when I started grieving for my mother and went through tough times.

My grandmother was the type of woman who talked to me at night and told me stories about my family's past. She told me about good things that happened to her in the past. She also told me *imigani,* which in English means proverbs. She wanted to tell me things that would be very important to me as I grew up. She always was telling me that she wanted to see me grow up, and sometimes now I still think, "I must be kind, because this is what my grandmother would want."

My grandmother was very generous. During the harvest season, anytime she had extra my grandmother gave to people who did not have anything. I remember how she liked the banana beer, and at night, if she did not have any made, she asked me to go get some from the store. Most of the time she wanted to have that beer ready to give people when they came to visit.

Grandmother was considered a mentor for many young women in our area. They came to her to ask advice about life or Christianity and things such as that. Many people came to her for advice and always liked to visit in her home. I remember children from the village came to stay the night, and I believe this impacted my life because it helped form my character. I think this is what people should be – living by example.

From the time I started becoming aware of things around me, my grandmother had a dog. The dog was my grandfather's pet and was very well-known. Very few people in Rwanda had dogs for pets like the American way – normally, just people who hunted or rich people living in the capital city had dogs for pets. My grandparents really loved the dog. His name was Jalu, and he was a Belgian shepherd. He died of old age when I was very young and I remember that my grandparents and neighbors adored the dog. He was protective of the house and went to the pasture with the cows.

My grandmother still had two sons, Diogene and Theogene, living at home when I came to live with her. Diogene was still attending school, but Theogene left to join the RPF in 1990.

Back then, you never told your mother or your grandmother that you were going to join the rebellion, because they would try to convince you not to go. They knew you could be killed on the way to the jungle where the rebellion members were living. Many young people went and joined the RPF, but they did not let their parents know about this.

We received a lot of news about kids who wanted to join the RPF, but who were caught by the government on their way and were killed. They were killed in a very inhumane way. I heard about one of my neighbors who joined and was caught. They killed him by burying him in a desert, but leaving his head above the ground. The birds would come and peck his eyes out. After this, parents were very worried. The government did this to discourage people from joining the rebellion.

Right after my uncle Theogene joined the RPF, the mayor of Ntarama (a Hutu) and the police came to us. They had guns and grenades. I just came home from school and was putting my books down, and I went looking for my grandmother. When I looked, my grandmother was outside on the front porch with the mayor and police. I did not know it was the mayor and I went outside and stood by her. The mayor had a long stick and pointed it at my grandmother, asking her, "Where is your son?" My grandmother started shaking and weeping, and said, "I don't know where my son is. I sent my son to school and I don't know where he is." The mayor said, "Tell us the truth. Tell us where your son is." My grandmother said, "No, my son is at school. If he is not, prove it." The mayor said, "No, your son has joined the RPF." My grandmother said, "No, my son did not join the RPF."

The men left, but the mayor said, "You will pay the consequence." They left and we stayed there, but we were very, very scared. Back then, there were no cell phones and no computers so she could not tell her children in the capital city. I do not know if she even shared with the neighbors, because you could be persecuted because of your tribe, even then.

After this, we started worrying and wondered what we were going to do – would we be kidnapped or killed? My grandmother was a very faithful Christian woman, and she would say, "God will keep us safe. There is nothing we can do." The men never came back.

On his way to school, my cousin Eric sneaked out to the jungle to visit the RPF and saw my uncle Theogene. He got pictures and brought them from the camp and that is when my grandmother realized it was true that my uncle had joined the RPF. Unfortunately, we lost those pictures during the genocide. (One of our employees took them and spread them in the street and people trampled them as they were running to escape. We would hear them say, "Oh, we saw your uncle's picture on the street," like it was joke.)

My grandfather had been dead many years by the time I was born and my grandmother managed the property. Sometimes this meant hiring help to do the work. She had a lot of land and cattle to take care of. She used my uncles to make sure that everything was managed well. There was plenty of land to grow food, and plenty of cows, which meant plenty of milk. She gave much of the responsibility for the cattle to one of my uncles who lived nearby. I believe my grandmother had plenty of money to help her survive.

My grandmother also had three men who were hired to help her – one was the "house boy," Nyakarundi, who took care of things in the house. He also took care of the agriculture and harvesting. He received a very small payment for his work. He was from Burundi and was a survivor of a war in Burundi, called Ntega-Namarangara. He came to Rwanda as a job hunter. There were many like him in my country at that time.

The other house boy had lived with my grandmother since before I was born, and was a Hutu named Karimwabo. His job was to cook and help with any other work that my mother would normally have done at home. He later betrayed us.

The third man, Twagira, was hired to help with the cows, and was from a village nearby. He was not paid, but received a cow each year that he worked for my grandmother, so by the end of ten years, he would have received ten cows.

My uncle Eugene, who was living near us, would stop by to do things that my grandmother could not do. Another uncle, Diogene, who was attending school, came over during vacation, and my cousins who lived nearby with their parents sometimes came and stay with Grandmother. During vacation there were always a lot of people around, which meant a lot of food.

Every time my grandmother was not around, I would stay with our "house boy" Nyakarundi. Sometimes he laid a mat of grass on the ground, and we sat down and shared stories. Because I was young, I saw him as someone who cared about me and I always paid attention to what he said. He was very kind, and he knew how to sing and play a musical instrument called an *umuduri*. The *umuduri* is a wire strung on a piece of curved wood, similar to a bow.

My other grandmother lived in the country about 10 miles away and sometimes I went to visit her. I went to school in the morning, and then I asked permission from grandmother to go spend the night with my other grandmother. When I went there, she cooked good food for me, and was always so happy to see me. My aunt Ufitinema, who was not married, lived with her and she also treated me as a son. She made sure I had good food and that I got to school. To get to and from her house, I would run.

From the time I was very young, one of my jobs was to care for the cows when the help was on vacation, or to go and make sure the help was doing the right things. This meant taking a herd of 30 or more animals and walking them to a pasture to eat, standing guard over them, and bringing them home. Rwandan cows are very large and most have long horns, much like the Texas Longhorn cattle. The horns can be trained to grow in whatever direction you chose, and many times I worked to bend the horns, and made them grow to where they pointed down or out or up. To take the cows to pasture, I walked through thorns that often pierced my feet. The cattle were kept in pens at night, to keep them from wandering off and roaming into neighbors' gardens or personal property. During the day, we took them to graze in pastures, sometimes on my grandfather's property and sometimes on common land. I developed different whistles to lead the cows. I had one whistle to call them to water, and another for them to follow me. The cows learned the whistle calls and responded to me. Sometimes, I also sang for the cows. I had one song for when they were drinking water, which was to give them an appetite for water, and another song to calm the cows when they were being milked.

Sometimes, during the dry season, when the grazing was not good, I took the cows to the neighbors' garden at night and let them eat the people's food. If anyone was caught doing this, he would be taken to the leader (the chief) and sometimes would have to go to court. If the court found them guilty, the victim was awarded compensation, and allowed to choose a cow from their herd.

Sometimes, when I took the cows home, my mother or grandmother said to me, "These cows are very hungry. Did you take them to the pasture today?" If the adults were mad at you, the answer was to take the cows at night to steal people's food (from the garden). Some nights when I took the cows out, the owner of the property had trained guard dogs. I learned if I whistled the dogs stopped. I also learned that if it is very dark where you go, no one can follow you!

Every day before I went to school, it was my job to go get water. The well was about ten miles from my home, so I woke up very early. Several of us woke up very early and went together. If you woke up before the others, you went to their house and got them. At that time, we knew no difference between Hutu and Tutsi. We sang on the way to the well, and told jokes. We woke up and ran to the valley to get the water, but went slowly coming back.

Also, in our culture, in general it was the kids' job to run errands, so if Grandmother needed something from the store, she sent me. Or if you wanted to communicate with your neighbor, you sent your kid. In our community, we had a wonderful culture of sharing, so if you needed a cooking pan, or a match, or a tool, you went to your neighbor. You did not ask, "Who is a Tutsi or who is a Hutu?" We just shared with everyone. Another job for kids was to go find wood used for cooking. The kids also took care of the animals.

In our village, we had dancing troops composed of kids. In the evenings, everyone gathered and sang and ate, and the kids danced. There were people who were interested in the dances who volunteered to teach the kids and the dances were handed down from generation to generation. Rwanda is well-known for traditional dances.

The kids also played games. One game was *gusakuza*, which involved asking trick questions and the others trying to find the answer. The older people also shared stories of the past and told parables.

We had metal wheels that were similar to bicycle wheels, and we chased these wheels through the streets with a stick. Doing this made you fast. We used this on any kind of mission we went on. If Grandmother wanted me to go to the store, I used the wheel. It was like a toy – a gift – and I took it with me everywhere. I did not consider running to be a career at this point in my life. Running was just the way you got from one place to another. I have many scars on my knees that came from running at that time of my life – from falling down. But I always got up and kept going.

As kids, on the weekends when there was no school, we grabbed buckets and lied to our parents, and said, "We are going to get water from the valley." In the valley, there were a lot of tomatoes planted. Instead of getting water, we hid salt and pepper and then we stole tomatoes and put salt on them and ate them. After we got full, we would go swim. There were dams in the river where the cows got water, so we could swim there. We got home very late, and some of us got in trouble and were beaten. You could get beaten and go to the hospital, and nobody cared. That is the way it still is because of the lack of education.

I never got in trouble, though, because my grandmother always protected me. Again, the Hutu and Tutsi were all together and there was no question of which tribe you belonged to.

In the evenings, we all went to play soccer. There was a field where the kids met. The games were for anyone – there was no discrimination there. We did not know anything was wrong, but obviously the adults knew there were some tensions.

If anyone had a wedding, everyone went – with or without an invitation. You just showed up, because we were all about community and what it could do for us. If someone was baptized across town, everyone went.

Most people lived off of agriculture, so there were only a few things, such as sugar, salt and tea, that you bought at the market. Most of the time you had sufficient food to eat at home, so we were a very, very happy people in my community.

I was well-known in my village because our house was right on a busy street, where people went by to go to the store, to church and to sports events. I stood on the street and called people by name. If I did not know them, I asked their name, and I had a good memory so I learned their first name and last name. I was also known because of my head. I had a big head, in terms of its size, so I was known as the kid with the big head. They called me *Rutwe* which means *Big Head*. People always knew if I was not on the street when they went by, I would be there when they came back.

No one in our village had a car, so if a business person came to pick up bricks, we heard the car coming from several miles away. When we heard a car come, we chased it, so that by the time the car got to the village all the kids from the area were chasing the car and running around it. I think this is another reason I was so fast at running. Because the streets were so bad, the cars drove very slowly and kids could climb on the car while it was moving, so the cars were covered with kids.

I remember one time we were chasing a car that was owned by one of the richest men from our area. We were just jumping trying to get on the car, and the man told everyone to get off the car, except me. He said, "I know his dad, and so if anything happens to him, it will be okay. But if anyone else gets hurt, no one will understand that it is not my fault."

I never had shoes to wear until I reached high school, which was very common in my country. Only the very rich people wore shoes - only those whose fathers were in the Army or those who were business men, who were very, very rich. I remember one time a kid was wearing shoes at my kindergarten school and we were all so surprised. This man came in and signed up his children to bring them to our school, and we were all so surprised when we saw him with shoes on. We thought he was walking funny. Not having shoes was not a shame, as it was very common.

Sometimes, when we sent the cows to the pasture there were things on the ground that would hurt you, such as stones, knives, pieces of metal, pins, etc. Sometimes it was muddy, and in the mud there were a lot of bacteria and diseases that could spread through that. When we were cut or wounded, we did not go to see a doctor or go to the hospital. Instead, we took small grasses or herbs and mixed them into a paste for a wound or a liquid if it was to drink. Whenever I had a cough or fever, my main medicine was herbs. I never went to the hospital. My grandmother was excellent at making medicines. We also had a lot of neighbors who were traditional doctors, so if my grandmother could not make a cure, my neighbors were able to.

I remember that one day I was bitten by a snake, and my grandmother did not know the herbs to cure snakebite, so she took me to a neighbor and I was able to get the herbs. I was bruised everywhere on my body, I was sweating and my mouth was dry from lack of saliva. After the medicine, I started to feel good. I drank a lot of milk and a lot of water. In fact, in my culture we believe that milk is medicine for thousands of sicknesses, so whenever anything happens we look for milk.

I never went to a doctor until I was around six or seven years old. I remember the first time I went to get a shot, which was an immunization shot, was when the French military was in my country and initiated a program to get immunizations to poor children in the area. This was the first time I went for immunizations, and it was thirty miles to get there. As kids, we had to walk to get the immunizations, and it was a very big deal. I remember that although we had to walk, we were very excited that we were going to see white people and they would give us shots. It was a long way, but we never felt it because we were so excited about going. I remember on our way there, we saw a French truck. We were so excited that we tried to climb onto the truck and get into it. I remember the kids trying to climb on the truck and the French army grabbed sugar cane and beat the children off the truck.

Most of the doctors and nurses in our country at that time were European, and so were white. Most of the nurses were nuns. Most of the school leaders, as well, were Europeans – usually nuns and priests. This meant Europeans were in charge of the education and the health sectors, and most of them were from the Catholic Church. So, most of the country was Christian, which is why the country was 99 percent Christian by the time of the genocide. I think the Catholic Church and the Europeans brought a lot of good things to my country. By bringing education, they brought infrastructure and medical care.

I started first grade when I was five years old. I remember that my grandmother called my cousin Eric and said, "Come and take Serge to school." I remember going to school and it was after 8 a.m., so everyone was already in class. We were late. You went to school and the teacher accepted you and you were in class. I went to my own class and my cousin went to his class. School was very new to me. It was very different. I did not know how to count. I did not know how to get along with kids that I wasn't used to. My first teacher was a Tutsi, and that made school easy. That semester, I was first in the class and did well with my grades. That was the only year I had a Tutsi for a teacher.

In the second grade, my scores dropped. I do not know if this was because the professor was Hutu, but it was known that a professor from a different tribe could fail you. It later became known that I failed because of my tribe. Later in second grade, my teacher was sick and he was replaced by another teacher. I remember that when the new teacher came, I got third in the class. Unfortunately, he was killed in the genocide. I remember passing by the street and seeing him lying on the ground with so many wounds. I was so shocked. Imagine having a teacher who was your hero and then seeing him lying on the ground. Seeing him like that made my mind go back and think of what a good relationship that I had with him. That is when I started to think about tribes and the hate that existed among us.

After my second grade is when the genocide began. That time of going to school is when the hate started. This is when you started to know that, "You are a Tutsi," "You are a Hutu," or "You are a Twa." Most of the teachers were Hutu, and we learned that the Hutu government would not hire Tutsi. The Twa really did not care about government, money or leadership, so there were not many of them in the schools.

The teachers brought the word from the government about separating the Tutsi and Hutu. I had a mean professor who came and said, "Hutu, stand up." Then he said, "Whoever is not standing up, go outside for a while." When you came back inside, if you made a small mistake, you would be beaten like a snake. I remember being beaten because I sat in a place where I wasn't supposed to sit. My teacher told me to go outside, and it was raining, raining, and I had to stand outside for two hours. The principal walked by and saw me outside. I thought he would see me and tell me to go inside, but he saw me and did not say anything. A teacher, who was a Tutsi, saw me standing outside and went to the professor and said, "I think the kid is going to get sick." So the teacher brought me inside, but he told me because I had not done the work, I would be punished. So he beat me with a stick and I had bruises on my leg. This was very common and some kids had even worse punishment. It was at this time that the hate started to grow through teachers, through kids, through officials.

I went home and told my grandmother about this. I think she did not want to traumatize me, so she did not talk about the hate, but just encouraged me to behave well at school. It was rough. You could do well in a class, and still be last in the class. I remember I was number one in the class for three semesters, and then I got a new teacher, and got zeroes in everything except for one subject. From that time on, all my teachers were Hutu, and so my grades were worse. My grandmother and my uncles were very unhappy and I could not explain what happened. It was not until much later in life that I realized what was going on.

Sometimes we went home after school, and the Hutu and Tutsi children were fighting each other because they got the hate from their parents. Kids fought on the way home from school, and kids were bruised or had broken bones from fighting. At that time, however, neighbors did not hate each other and did not show hate. They still shared meals with each other.

A little bit before 1990, the war started and people started killing each other randomly. The killings were planned throughout Rwanda ahead of time. Rwandese Abatutsi refugees, who had fled to Uganda in 1959, tried to organize attempts to rescue the victims because they heard the attacks were coming. People from Rwanda, Congo, Burundi, Tanzania, Uganda, Kenya and a few from other African countries joined the RPF.

The hate where neighbor turned against neighbor did not come out until the genocide. Some people were being trained behind the scenes about killing. We knew that young kids were being trained in how to kill. Bananas were used for training to kill. Kids were given machetes and taken to banana trees, and told to cut the tree and see how fast they could cut them.

I remember one day I went to get water from the public tub, and a group was having a meeting by the water tub. There were police and soldiers and party leaders, and a police officer grabbed me and said, "Oh, you are a snake!" He put me in his truck and said, "Stay there." I was crying, and he said, "Go home and don't say anything." I went home and did not say anything because it was a party meeting.

The Tutsi were referred to as "snakes" and "tall trees." The term "snake" came from the Bible where God said that man would have rule over the serpent, and we were considered as the Hutu's enemies. Also, as a snake is considered very dangerous, they also considered the Tutsi to be very dangerous. The Hutu also called us tall trees because the Tutsi are very thin and tall, with tall, sharp noses. All these ideas came from the Belgian and German colonists, who started measuring the nose size. The Belgian and German colonists also said that the Tutsi came from the Nile region of Egypt, and did not consider us to be Rwandese. During the genocide, the Hutu considered us to be Egyptian, and they threw people into the Nile River, and said, "Hey, go back to where you came from."

I remember during the genocide, a young couple, who were newlyweds, being killed. They put them together and put a sharp stick through them, from one person to the next person, and threw them in the river, and said, "Go back to where you came from."

My grandmother was a very religious woman, and a devout Catholic. She was a very strong Christian and an example to me and the village. I remember her waking up at 5 a.m. on Sunday mornings, to pray and say her rosary. She made sure I went to church every Sunday. During school time, it was mostly my grandmother and me and my mother. Grandmother expected all her family to attend church and they were there when they came home during the summer. I remember sitting on the front row at church. The first row was right by the door, and if anyone went by the door during church they were able to see me.

Because of my habit of sitting in the front row, after the church was bombed in the genocide, when my family came looking to see if I was killed too, they immediately went to the front row.

We were so impressed by the white priests, because then most of the priests were from Europe, and they looked so different from us. I always wanted to touch a white person's skin, to see how it felt. The priests knew that, and told us, "Of course you can touch us." They knew it would make us happy and laugh. We thought they talked funny because they were trying to speak Kinyarwanda, and with their accents it sounded funny to us. But we liked it and were impressed that they wanted to learn our language. As a kid, I wanted to sit close to the priests.

The priests had very big farms, and sometimes before church they brought fruit and gave it to the kids, or they brought balls to us and it was lots of fun. After the genocide, I was also an altar boy because I thought that was cool.

These church leaders also owned a large part of the land, which they received during colonial times. The schools and hospitals lived off the land because they were able to grow food. If you got a job with the Catholic Church you were well-respected because of the power the church possessed. A few of my neighbors worked at the headquarters of the Catholic Church in my province, and we thought they knew everything and that they were very powerful. Some Rwandans, many of them Hutu, became leaders in the Catholic Church and attained high positions within the diocese, so during the genocide even the leaders in the church were guilty of the killing.

During the genocide, some of the priests took part in the killing, and others hid people. I remember one sister, Antonio, was hiding some Tutsi who were going to be killed by the government. The government came at night and killed her. Also, some priests were accused of committing genocide and this is still an ongoing process. Some of them fled to Europe, and some of them are still in hiding and travelling around the world. Some are being protected by other nations. Some have been prosecuted and are serving jail time, and some are still being hunted by the Rwandan government and United Nations.

Serge Gasore and the child of his neighbor, following a baptism in the child's family.

Mujawamariya Beate – mother of Serge Gasore

THE GENOCIDE

Day 1: The genocide began on April 6, 1994, after the Hutu president's airplane crashed. This is when the Hutu began saying to the Tutsi, "You killed our president." It was just an excuse; they were already planning to kill us. The Hutu used the president's death as justification to begin the slaughter. I know they were planning to kill us because I watched at the place where the high-school and middle-school students were being trained to kill people. The Hutu began stockpiling machetes from Japan and making plans. Our teachers told us that the conflict must continue. They encouraged us to hate each other. Most of these teachers were Hutu.

News of the plane crash was on the radio that evening. Hutu radio station *Radio Télévision Libre des Mille*

Collines (RTLM)[3] began saying things like, "Let's kill the cockroaches," and "It is time to cut down the tall trees." They said to cut down the tall trees because they said the Tutsi were tall and thin. They also said things like, "Beware of the snake. When you see one, kill it, because if you don't kill it, it will kill you." The radio station had an announcer, Noheri, who was later killed while on the air. He taunted the Rwandan Tutsi, saying, "The rabbits are coming, let's kill them. They have ears and tails like dogs." While he was talking, a bomb came through the roof of the radio station and killed him. Noheri and others on the radio incited and encouraged the violence.

The Hutu immediately set fire to Tutsi houses. All night long on April 6 and 7, Tutsi homes burned in my village. The radio announcers warned everyone to stay in their houses, and the Hutu took advantage of this by burning the houses. The people who could went and hid, but old people and young children were burned in their homes.

---

3   The station's name is French for "One Thousand Hills Free Radio and Television", deriving from the description of Rwanda as *"Land of a Thousand Hills"*. It received support from the government-controlled Radio Rwanda, which initially allowed it to transmit using their equipment. Widely listened to by the general population, it projected racist propaganda against Tutsi, moderate Hutu, Belgians, and the United Nations mission UNAMIR. It is widely regarded as having played a crucial role in creating the atmosphere of charged racial hostility that allowed the genocide to occur. A November 2009 study by a PhD candidate at the Institute for International Economic Studies of Stockholm estimated that the broadcasts explained an increase in violence that amounted to 45,000 Tutsi deaths, about 9% of the total." "Radio Television Libre Des Mille Collines." *Wikipedia*. Wikimedia Foundation, 29 Nov. 2013. Web. May 2012.

Tensions and plans were building since 1987, but the president's plane crash was the catalyst that set it all in motion. Everything was very crazy, people were all trying to run away, there was smoke everywhere, and I heard people screaming for help. Everyone was running in different directions. Many met at schools or at churches looking for refuge.

The first thing I remember about the genocide was at night. We were about to go to bed. My grandmother liked to listen to a radio station that broadcasted from the jungle because it was a RPF radio station. Many Tutsi listened to this radio station to get the truth about what was going on. The national radio station gave wrong information, and said such things as the RPF were killed, etc. The RPF radio station was called *Muhabura*, and if you listened to this station, you had to hide, because if Hutu neighbors or the army doing patrol heard you, you could be killed or tried in court. I remember my grandmother listening to that station, and before she listened she closed the windows and doors, and made sure no one was around. We were very scared.

The day of the president's plane crash, it happened that my uncle Diogene was home from school. My cousin Simba and myself and the house boy, Karimwabo, were there, too. We knew that the airplane crashed. My grandmother was old and she was smart and she told me it was going to get bad, that we were going to be in trouble.

We heard the news on the national radio that the president's plane was shot by "cockroaches" and then they used a lot of other words to scare people. We were very confused and had no means of communicating with other members of the family. We heard the sounds of gunfire coming from the capital city. The RPF sent armies to the capital city for peace talks and immediately after the president's plane was shot, the Hutu began to target the armies in the capital city and the RPF began fighting against the government forces.

Since we did not know what was happening, we ended up going to bed. I went to bed and was supposed to go to school in the morning. I was very happy as a kid, and excited that the president was dead because I heard other people complaining about him, so I was partying in my heart. I saw in the eyes of my uncle, my cousin and my grandmother that they were very frightened and afraid that something bad was going to follow. Because I was a kid, I did not think much about the consequences of having the president killed.

When we woke up in the morning, it was time to go to school, and being an ignorant kid, I grabbed a bucket to go get water as usual. On my way to get water, I met a guy named Gregor, who worked at the Catholic head-quarters in our area, and he said, "Serge, where are you going?" I told him, "I am going to get water so I can take a shower and go to school." When I met him, he was on his way to his house. He had been on his way to work, but on the way the militia told him to go home. They had roadblocks on the street, and had the power to tell him to go back. He said, "Serge, I was going to work, but they told me I cannot work today because the president was killed. You must stay home and not come out." I went home, still celebrating because the president was dead. My grandmother told me no, that this was going to be bad.

We decided to leave the house and go listen to the news on the radio with our Tutsi neighbors. We went there, but the Hutu neighbors did not come – they stayed in their house. To listen to that radio station, we went in the house and closed the windows and doors, and some men stayed outside and stood watch. We stayed there until around 3 p.m. Our house was right by the street, but the neighbor's house was a little higher up on the mountain and you could see what was happening on the other side of the town. We saw large numbers of people coming, walking by crying, with their goats, cows, pigs, their mattresses on their heads. Everything that belonged to them, they had on their heads. They were coming from the area where we were. As soon as we saw them, we looked away from where we were, and we saw houses being burned. I remember a woman saying, "My son was burned, and my goats were burned in the house, too. I do not know where my husband went."

People were crying and screaming, and that is when I started to realize the truth. In my heart, I said, "I think we are going to see something wrong." We stayed in our neighbor's house until later in the evening and then we went home. The people who walked by the house went and camped in the Catholic Church. The street was too small for people, because there were all those goats, pigs, people – everyone and everything trying to run away. We slept in our house.

Day 2: When I woke up the morning of April 7, I took a bucket to go get some water from my neighbor. On my way I met a leader from the church, a Tutsi named Gregoire. He told me the president had died and that we were waiting to die too. I remember he said, "Maybe you won't die Serge, because God is on your side." I got scared and ran back home instead of getting water. My dad was in Kigali, which is the capital city of Rwanda, and I was in the village with my grandmother.

My neighbors, who were Hutu, had a big family with some girls and some boys. Some of them were also former soldiers for the Hutu government. When we woke up in the morning we saw them leave. The kids and their mom and sisters stayed home, but two guys left. Other members of the family were not present because they were married and lived in different parts of the country. The two guys who were there left with machetes and spears. We did not think too much about it, because we knew we were different. They did not come to where we were, and they did not seem worried about what was going on. I remember in the evening I was standing on the street around 6 p.m. and I saw Celestin, one of the guys. He came and walked by the house with a machete in his hand and some meats in a small plastic bag. He made jokes, saying, "Oh, Serge, we had a lot of meats today. We had a lot of fun today." He made jokes to me. I saw the machete had blood everywhere, but I was nervous and scared enough not to ask him why the blood was on the machete. Even though I was young, I knew not to ask him about it. He said, "Tomorrow, we are going to get more meat and I will bring you some livers." He knew that my favorite meat was liver. Now, I know that he got the meat after they killed people and took their cows, and that some of that blood on the machete could have been human blood. When he said that, "Tomorrow we are going to go back and have fun again," something in my mind said, "Tomorrow you are going to kill more people." I remember he cleaned his machete by rubbing it on the wet grass. After he left, I went and told my grandmother about this and told her that Celestin had a lot of meat and he said he would bring us some tomorrow. My grandmother got mad and told me to "shut up." After that, I did not see Celestin. I know that he died after the genocide, and I heard that he was killed by the people whose families he had killed.

A young man in that family was my best friend. We spent a lot of time together, eating together, playing together, etc. If my grandmother could not find me, she knew I was with him and if his family could not find him, they knew he was with me. It was very interesting how in one second they stopped that kid from coming to us and that relationship was broken and there was no more relationship. Three months after the genocide, I met him in Kigali and he was selling charcoal. I went up to him and said, "Hey, Gatashya, do you remember me?" He looked at me, and said, "No." He said, "I don't remember you, are you from Bugesera?" I said, "Yes, don't you remember the little kid that you used to play with?" He said "No, I really don't remember." That's when I thought that he was probably guilty about what his family did to us. I saw him again many years later, and we were able to talk and have good conversation. I hope to find him again someday and be able to develop a relationship.

Day 3: Early in the morning on the third day, on my way back from getting water, I saw many fires, Tutsi people with mattresses, children crying and people fleeing with their belongings. I told my grandmother what I saw and she said, "Let's be ready to move out." She took our important things, such as pictures and things we valued, and buried them in the ground. Our house boy, Karimwabo, the Hutu who had worked for us a long, long time, helped us do this. We thought he was a nice guy because he was with us for a long time and was a mentor to many people. We dug a big hole and put everything under the ground and then put grass over it. When we left, he dug up our things and scattered them all around the area.

People were dying around the country, so my grandmother, along with my uncle Diogene and my cousin Simba, decided to go to the church. My grandmother prepared food to take with us. She prepared a banana dish and put it in a small container, and we took things to milk our cows because they were going with us. We took our mattress, too.

My grandmother had someone she had adopted as her son a long time before this. He occasionally visited our house. He was there with us, and he asked my grandmother to leave him in the house. No one really knew if he was a Hutu or Tutsi. We left him in the house and locked it, and when we came back, the house was still locked, but he was gone. However, nothing was missing from the house.

My grandmother and other family members and I left our houses to go hide in the church. We believed that no one would kill us in the place of Christ. When we got to the church, my uncle Diogene decided to leave. We did not know if he wanted to join the RPF or if he wanted to find his own safe place. He asked my grandmother for money to take a boat. He asked for FRW (Franc[s] Rwanda) 400 (less than $1) and my grandmother told him, "I don't have money," and asked him where he was going. I do not know if he told her where he was going. He left with a spear he could use if he got caught.

My cousin Eric had a long knife he grabbed to use in case he was attacked by the Interahamwe militia. (The Interahamwe militia was made up of civilian people who had received military training and were given weapons to kill the Tutsi, and the moderate Hutu, who were not on their side.) Immediately, my uncle Diogene disappeared, so it was just me, my cousins Runyonga and Simba, and my grandmother, who went and joined the other people at the Catholic Church.

During the whole time of the war, my cousin Simba never wanted to stay with the crowd. He always had a tactic of going where the killers had already been, which kept him safe for a while. For those of us at the church on the third day, everything was okay. We stayed there, prayed to God, and those who had milk drank it. We milked our cows, and my uncles Eugene and Athanase, who lived near us, had their cows there as well. That day was good.

While we were at the church, we had a system of going back to the house very early in the morning, grabbing whatever we had in the garden, cooking it and getting back to the church before 9 a.m. because the killers' schedule was 9 a.m. to 5 p.m. We ate whatever we found. That morning when we went to get what we could to eat, we checked on what we buried in the ground, and everything was gone. All the pictures we buried were scattered in the street, and that is what told us the house boy dug them up. We heard that he joined the militia, and many of our friends told us they saw him in the killing group.

In my mind, as a kid, I knew now that things were going to get really bad. Someone I took as my inspiration had turned against us and took our stuff. I asked myself,

"Where is the adopted one that my grandmother and grandfather have invested in and now he is gone?"

On the third day, the militia was busy killing people who could not leave their houses. These were old people and people with young children and infants who could not reach the church. We were safe for that day. However, on that day at 2 p.m. a group of killers came and surrounded us with traditional weapons, which were machetes and sticks that had nails on the end (called ubuhiri), arrows, swords, hammers and any other thing made of sharp metal. The killers came from different areas – some from the north, some from the south, some from the east and some from the west. A group of us tried to defend ourselves and stood in front of them with the weapons we had. In our tradition, most men had to have some sort of tool at home that they could use to defend themselves. I remember being outside, not being involved, but being where I could watch what was going on. I remember a man standing in front of this group of many people with a bow and arrow. He drew back the bow and everyone ran away. Every one of us was very proud of him for how he turned them back. The killers were very scared of dying – they wanted to kill, but they were afraid to die.

Day 4: On the fourth day following the president's death, we woke up as usual and went to get something to eat. We heard that my uncle Diogene, who had run away, was trapped and surrounded by killers in a bamboo bush. They told us there was no chance for him to survive. This news came to us from one who had escaped that attack. My grandmother was very worried that her son was going to die. But she was a Christian and a very strong woman, and she said in a quiet way, "Serge, let's go to the church."

A lot of people who were very serious about Christianity were at the church. Many of these were women, old men, children and the handicapped. They stayed inside and prayed and sang, and said their rosary. The church was very small – maybe about 1700 square feet, and there were maybe 500 to 1000 people in it. Imagine the people in there who had hope that they were safe, because they hoped the killers would not come inside the church.

I remember being outside playing with other kids, and an army truck came to a group of old men who were considered by us to be very wise men. The army came and asked these men to come and sit down by the area where we went to get water. The army told them, "You are the ones leading the rebellion." These men tried to explain to the army that they were not causing trouble. The army men left and we could tell they were very mad, and we knew things were going to get very bad right away. As soon as they left, what seemed like thousands and thousands of militia came. Things started getting crazy. Our men fought against them, and I remember some of our men coming into the church with bullet wounds in their heads. I remember my cousin Eric telling me some of his friends were dead, and other people there were saying that their friends were dead. The men who tried to protect us were killed when the killers came outside the church.

I was very tired, so I went inside and lay against my grandmother's thigh. I was excited that I was in the church and felt safe. I thought I was in heaven. I was asleep on my grandmother's lap when the Hutu killers came to the Catholic Church. Hearing people say that we were being attacked and thinking that finally our time on the earth was over was a hard thing to understand, especially knowing we were in the house of God. It did not take me long to realize that I wasn't safe in the church because I heard grenades coming in and children screaming. I bet people who were old enough, by that time, knew that the church could be attacked because they were exposed to the story of Jesus enough to know that Jesus was attacked and died on the cross despite the fact that he was the son of God, and He had greater power than any of those people in the church had. My grandmother also realized that something was going to happen. I could tell that there were many thoughts in my grandmother's mind because of the way she prayed by saying her rosary over and over in her last minutes. She lost comfort in her chair and walked to the front of the church to meet others who were praying near the altar at the front of the church. During that transition from the seats to the altar there was no conversation because by that time the killing had already started in the church. However, I still saw her trying to use non-verbal communication to tell me that she loved me no matter what happened. If anyone has lived with grandparents you might be able to relate to this, because a grandparent's love is never absent, no matter what the situation. During a moment of silence I recalled when we were home during peaceful time and my grandmother said, "I wish God will not call me home anytime soon so I will see you growing up." That is what many parents think when they look at their kids or grandkids, and I could not believe that what she did not want was about to happen. As she made her way to the altar, bullets were flying and I saw them hit people and people fall. Many people began praying. People were shaking and confused and running into each other. They were falling on top of each other. The Hutu threw a grenade into the church. The grenade hit and my grandmother fell. I was behind my grandmother. She fell down and her blood splattered on my clothes. I had some blood in my mouth. Tasting a human being's blood, and knowing that you are the next person to die is the very last thing you would ever wish, or not at all. I thought I would die too, so I tried to find a way to escape. I thought that the sky was falling on me and the whole world was fighting against us or has abandoned us, because I smelled blood mixed with the milk we carried to the church for breakfast, lunch and dinner. I smelled guns and bullet's powder. After seeing my grandmother lying there, with her body divided into parts by a grenade, I lost my mind and said, "Basi," which in Swahili means, "That is enough."

I went through a window and out away from the church. There was a fence around the church, and as I got outside from the church I saw that the fence was broken and there was a hole in it. I ran. People were falling down; people were screaming and being cut on the neck and cut many times on their bodies. I was facing the fence and all of a sudden by chance I got through the fence. I thought I could cross the street and into a field where food was growing. There was a policeman (a sniper) who was shooting people. The policeman saw me and attacked me. He saw me from far away and shot at me. By then, blood was everywhere – in my ears, in my mouth. I thought I was bleeding, but it was my grandmother's blood.

I was running, running. I was running with my grandmother's dead body in my mind. I kept thinking of how she taught me to respect everybody regardless of who they were or where they came from, and she taught me to always work hard and maintain honesty, because at the end of the day it is not about you, instead it is about what you did for others. I kept running.

The fields were terraced, with frequent ditches in the ground to collect water when it rained in order to control erosion. As I ran through the field, the ground was wet, and I slipped on some poop and fell into one of those ditches, so the police lost their target. I passed out, and when I woke up I began running toward where I went to school for the first grade. Instead of stopping there, I kept running toward a valley. Everywhere around me, many people were running, there was no talking, everyone was trying to save their lives. We were like a group of ants trying to run away from a spray of insecticide. Some of those who ran away from the church stayed at the school, but the militia did not pursue anyone further than the church on that day.

I ran into a banana field. When the banana leaves move, they make a lot of noise and when they shake you can think that someone is after you. In the banana field, I heard voices and I ran to the group of people. I found that they were from my tribe, and I was so happy to see them. I thought, "Maybe I am going to be safe today."

In all the hours seeking a place to hide, I thought about the my grandmother's death and my neighbors I left dying in the church we once called a safe haven, the church where European priests and missionaries came to preach the good news of the Gospel. Before the genocide, our village symbolized heaven in my perspective and I still believe that God is working there. Until today, almost twenty years since the genocide, I live with the vision of my grandmother's dead body and that will haunt me forever. Also, sometimes I do not believe that she died.

In the valley were a lot of tall bamboo reeds that many people could hide in, so the group I joined moved into the valley. In the movie *Sometimes in April*, they filmed the exact place where we hid. When we were hidden, the Tutsi began helping each other hide and escape. We moved together that whole day into the bamboo bush. When I got into the bamboo bush, I almost lost my life. The ground was very soft where the bamboo grew, and during the day when we were walking, everything was okay because we could see the bad ground, but at night, when I could not see, it was easy for me to get trapped because it was muddy. I kept struggling and a lot of times the older men grabbed me and got me out. I would almost fall asleep because it was night and dark. The group would realize that I had fallen behind, and then they would come back to get me. One time they had gone on for maybe a couple of miles before they realized I was behind.

Day 5 and beyond: From the bamboo bush, we wanted to go out and see if anyone survived the bombing at the church. The bamboo was very tall, so if you were inside you could not tell where you were. Every time we guessed and tried to come out of the bush, we came out where the militia were having parties and celebrating. Finally, in the morning around 6 a.m., when the sun started to rise, we saw where we could go to find our way out. We walked toward the church. In their minds, most of the group wanted to go straight to another jungle area to hide and survive the rest of the killing, but in my mind and the minds of a few others, we wanted to go back to the church to see if there was anyone to rescue.

After walking around for about four hours, I found my cousin Eric, who had also been in the church during the bombing. So many people were hiding in the bamboo bush and there was such chaos, at first I did not even see him. When my cousin Eric and I found each other in the valley, we decided to go back to the church after the killers left to see who died and who was alive. When we got to the church, we found two of my cousins from my aunt who lived nearby – two girls, Francine and Diane. They were in the street. I asked them how they were, and they said "good," but they were covered with blood. They told me not to go to the church, because they said that everyone was killed. When I got to the church, I saw that many of my family and relatives had died. The killers took all my relatives who were killed and put them in a pile together. They were able to do this, because the killers were people who knew you – they were your friends and your neighbors before the genocide began. They stacked the bodies of my family and relatives, and other dead Tutsi up in the front of the church. All of my relatives killed that day were Tutsi - Rukara Jean Claude, my cousin, the son of my uncle Athanase (my father's brother), my cousin Cadet, my aunt Agnes' daughter, and many others.

When I went in the church, I heard one of my aunt Agnes' daughters, Laura, screaming. She was young and weak and the bodies fell on top of her and she could not get out. I moved the bodies to get her out. I took her to the school where everyone was, and my cousin Simba was there as well. He was overwhelmed to find out I was still alive. For everyone, because they knew how close I was to my grandmother, in their minds, when she was killed they thought I was killed too, and so I was no longer in their minds.

My uncle Theogene, who disappeared when we went to the church, finally appeared on that day, in the evening, and we were all so happy and celebrating. He was skinny as a stick and we never asked him where he had been. My grandmother was gone and he had to grieve for her, but he could not grieve because so many people died that it was just normal and like you were just there waiting to die.

AT THE SCHOOL

All of those who survived the bombing at the church, and people who came from other areas of town, met for shelter at the school I had attended for first grade. By this time, our faith was gone. We believed that we did not deserve life, because if anyone could go inside a church and kill people, there were no more ways for anyone to survive. We decided that we would defend ourselves to the last minute. We decided that those who were able to go fight would go fight, and the small boys who could not fight would pick up stones that the others could use as weapons. On that day, we tried to go and make a roadblock so that the killers could not reach the camp. I did not go, but most of those who were older than I was went. This included my uncle Athanase, who was Eric's dad, and my other uncle Eugene and my aunt's husband and my cousin Simba. They went to fight so they could keep the fighting away from us.

Many of them lost their lives fighting the militia, but they also killed some of the militia during the fighting. Every time they came back, we saw so many people with wounds. Many were bleeding and some died. We buried those whose bodies we found, but many of their bodies could not be found, so we had to just forget about them.

The next day, the same thing happened, and we received many attacks from every direction. The attacks were a way to try to defeat us because we defended ourselves. We fought the first day and we won. The second day, we won. The third day, we won. The fourth day, I remember that we struggled. We had to run a little and move from the school. However, when it was the militia's time to go back for the day, they left and we were able to go back to the school.

On a normal day at the "concentration camp," which was how we referred to the school, as we got used to the killers' schedule, we woke up about 9 a.m., we gathered our stuff and got ready to run, expecting the killing to be over by 5 p.m. Normally, we never expected to live to reach the next minute, so this was just a dream. Families that had strong people gave us food before we started running. They would go get their livestock. If they had goats, they would try to take them and hide them as far away as they could. Every time we came from hiding, we would run, run, run until 5 p.m. If you survived in the bush until 5 p.m., then you headed back to the camp.

You knew it was 5 p.m. without a watch, because if you saw a helicopter above you, that meant it was 5 p.m. The government used the helicopter to see how many people survived and how many people were killed, to know how to plan their mission for the next day. Another sign was hearing shots in the air. One shot let the killers know that it was time to head back to their houses. The reason they shot in the air was to make sure they all moved at the same time and no one was left behind to be killed by us. Once the killers headed home, we also went back to our concentration camp. A lot of times we went back to see if anyone was still alive or to see if anyone from our families was killed or wounded so that we could take care of them or bury them.

In our culture, it was not normal to eat our livestock, but when we started realizing that we did not have enough livestock to care, we started eating our goats or our cows. The killers took and ate most of our livestock. At that time, though, after 5 p.m. we gathered the leftover livestock and slaughtered it and cooked it as our meal.

I remember that my bed, like so many other people's beds, was on a hill outside the school. The bed was on stones just on top of the hill. We used tree leaves to make a bed and lay there the whole night. It was very cold and windy. After we ate the meats that were not even cooked well, we just stayed there wishing that the night would go fast. Even now, I can smell the smell of those meats and the smoke. In the morning we tried to wake up as soon as possible and get ready to move on.

By this time, many of those who could fight were dead, so we had no more power. We did not have any way to fight because we did not have guns – all we had were hunting materials and stones, although the militia had weapons. I remember working so hard, pushing stones on a wheelbarrow. Women from my tribe carried stones in their clothes. We tried so hard to get enough stones to the front for our soldiers to use. I remember trying to get the stones to the front, and on my way there I saw so many who were hurt and bleeding. We received some intervention coming to help fight against the killers, and the killers left. When the killers left the school, there was still some fighting going on in other areas and all our guys were killed.

One day, I remember taking stones on the wheelbarrow and as I dumped the stones the fighting guys were just right in front of me. All our guys were dead or wounded and our men were all defeated at that time. Men were lying on the ground screaming or dying. I remember them falling in front of me as I was dumping the stones, and the killers came so close to me that I could not stop at all. Then, a woman ran past me trying to reach some of our guys. This woman was in front of the killers, and she had a sign that said, "I am coming to get my wedding goods." This sign showed their intention was to come and get our stuff and take it for their own use.

I remember we were hiding at the kindergarten school and a group of killers came and threw grenades and had traditional weapons. That group came in to the school and killed some of us. I was also attacked. After they came across the room, some of the men fought back and ran after them. I was running away and I met the Interahamwe on its way to kill some Tutsi. I fell as I ran away and they caught me. They saw me and they asked me, "Who are you?" I stood up and started walking toward them (the killers). I thought they would kill me, but I thought that maybe if I lied and said that I was a Hutu they would let me live. I was scared. I said in my heart, "I am going to lie, because it is the only way I can survive" They said, "Where are you from?" "Who is your dad?" I thought, "I am going to say the name of a militia man and that way they will let me survive." So, I gave them the name of this person, and they said, "Okay," and let me go and told me to make sure that I did not get attacked.

I left and kept moving forward. I was searching for food on the ground, but then I ran into another group of killers. This group of men had different tools to kill the people. They saw me from far away and we ran into each other. I heard tambourines and saw a woman who was to be married the next day. She led the group and carried a sign that said she was coming to get something to bring to her house for a marriage. She was the same woman I saw earlier and she had a machete.

I tried to run away, but they chased me —screaming, whooping, and banging tambourines. They sang a song about the political party and they asked where I was coming from. They put me down on the ground and they got a stick with nails pointing out of it and they beat me in the head. I still have many scars from this beating. When I was nearly dead, they said, "Okay, let him die, others will kill him." They left. As they were leaving, the woman came back and said, "Oh, let me leave something with him. I want to give him a souvenir." She got a knife and cut the front of my shin and then she left. I still have that scar also. Before this happened, I never thought about women as soldiers or that they would be involved in the fighting. My image of women had always been that they were very nice and I had never thought they could act crazy like that.

After they left, I could not move for a while until it got dark and the sun was no longer hot. I was bleeding and I was sure I would die. I kept lying there, and then I moved to the banana trees. When it got dark, I was able to walk slowly back to the camp at the school where other Tutsi were hiding. When I got there, they fed me and washed my head, but there was no medicine. By that time, many people were killed at the school. My cousin Eric was still alive, but my uncle was wounded. He was shot in the hip. However, most of my family who had survived the church slaughter was still alive.

The next day, I was still recovering from being beaten in the head. There was fighting just like the day before. Many more were killed and it was a long day. In the evening, I went to the battle to cheer for those who were fighting. At the time I got there, our guys were just defeating the killers, and I remember seeing the same woman who had left me with the scar. I recognized her because I remember seeing the sign on her. I remember later, walking by the school where the fighting had taken place, and seeing her body lying in the street.

The killers kept attacking us and one day that I will never forget in my life, very early in the morning the killers came as mad as they had ever been. They came very early while we were all sleeping outside. They brought a soldier and he was able to sneak into our camp and climb into a tree. He climbed very high into the tree, taking with him a huge metal container that had a lot of bullets in it. We woke up in the morning and went about our normal morning activities, and were very shocked because the soldier in the tree could see everything happening on the ground. He was shooting people with a handgun, and you could hear bullets coming over your head. You woke up, came out of the school building, and got shot. He was shooting old women and children and anyone else he saw. At that time, we were very surprised and did not know what to do. This person was shooting and we could not see him.

Those people who were fighting against the killers were in a state of confusion because they could not see him, and this created confusion in the camp. At the same time, other attacks came from other locations – from the north, south, east and west. You can imagine how confusing this was. After that, some of our heroes did as much as they could to find the soldier who was shooting from the tree. They finally found him in the tree. When they found him, as they were approaching him, he shot them. Of course, this was easy for him as he was in a good position to shoot them. Many people, wise men and young people, died at that time because they were trying to attack him, but he was in a superior position. One of our men managed to shoot him in the leg with an arrow. Then, we heard him as he was struggling with the arrow, and another man shot him in the chest. He fell to the ground from the tree and everything fell apart. He died immediately, and we all shared his clothes. We were not used to soldiers, so this was something big for us. Touching the uniform of a soldier was something unusual, and we felt it was a big achievement to kill him, because he had killed many people. If you managed to get just a piece of his shirt, or even a button, you were very happy. I remember seeing one person walking by with one of the soldier's shoes and another person had another of his shoes. It was like when Jesus died and people shared his clothes. We shared the soldier's clothes.

Two things that we did not touch were the gun and the bullets. There was a man who was a driver for the police and he learned how to use a gun while driving for the police. In that whole area he was the only person who knew how to use a gun, so he got the gun.

After that we felt the sky fell on us. The government in the capital city heard that the soldier was killed and within 30 minutes, hundreds and hundreds of soldiers came to our concentration camp. It was raining very hard. They came in big buses. One thing I remember is seeing buses in line, driving toward our camp. It was a moment of confusion for everyone. We did not know what to do because guns were sounding everywhere. One thought was to run toward the bamboo bush, and that is where everyone headed. In that moment of confusion, I remember running and people around me were falling down like trees or leaves. As I looked behind me, people were falling down. As I looked to the side, people were falling down. Men were falling down, children were falling down. People were screaming. I thought the sky was falling down on me. I managed to get to the bamboo bush safely, but I thought that no one in my family was still alive.

When I got to the bamboo bush, I stayed there until 4:30 in the evening, and then I started moving back to the camp, as usual, because I knew the killers were about to head back to enjoy our belongings, such as cows, goats and chickens. When I got to the school, many of my relatives were wounded so badly. My aunt Agnes was wounded, her husband, Cyprian, was wounded for a second time, and my uncle Athanase was wounded so badly. Athanase was wounded at the fighting front, which was at the school. I remember that for several attacks, he was the one who woke me up when the killers came. I remember one day we were just finishing eating a turkey, and he heard the killers coming and he woke me up. Coming back from the bamboo bush and finding him wounded was a sad moment for me. I knew that he would never be able to fight again. Athanase decided to hide closer to the camp. My friends and I walked around the camp among the dead bodies seeing if we knew anyone. We knew most of them, as they were close to us. I remember walking by many dead bodies and I saw this small Bible (it was New Testament) and I wanted to grab it because I thought it would be good to have it. My friend said, "Serge, oh if you take that Bible, God will punish you."

We were all weakened by that attack. Around 6 p.m., we received another attack, which was unusual to be attacked at that time. This attack was led by a business man that we had all known. He attacked us with grenades and, unfortunately for him, he did not have the skills to use grenades. He wanted to throw the grenades at us, but they turned at him and he was wounded and he was killed by his group right away. The group managed to take his car and drove away. We did not know where they went. After that, we had a sad moment and everyone was quiet. It was very cold, and we went to sleep on our hill. We could tell that our camp was not safe anymore. The next morning, we knew that even if we were attacked, we would have to move to the bamboo bush as our third location, as the school was no longer safe.

We hid during the time the killers were searching. They came at 9 in the morning and killed until 5 p.m. and then went back to their camps. They stayed in a camp and woke up in the morning for training and exercise and then went and checked the bush and villages. They found Tutsi along the way who were too old or too young to flee and killed the Tutsi as they came to them. Then they moved on and looked for those Tutsi who were in hiding.

We moved to the bamboo bush, but my uncle Athanase was too badly wounded during the first two attacks at the school and had to hide near the school. He did not have a chance to escape because he was too old. He thought that he could go and hide in one of the burned out houses because the Hutu killers would think everyone was already dead and would not check there.

The Interahamwe found uncle Athanase where he was hiding. He was first attacked on the morning of April 7, 1994. The first day they found him, they cut off part of one leg and poked out his eyes and left him to die. The Interahamwe came back every day and cut another part of his arm, and cut his arms and legs further up, along with different parts of his body.

Eric remembered his father said he was going to try to hide in one of the burned out houses, so we went to find him. This is when we found him cut so badly. Eric and I were hiding in the bush together and went in to check on his father every day when we were sure the killers were gone. We kept checking on him each day, until he died. There was nothing we could do for him because he was already so badly injured and we were young. (My cousin was 12 years old and I was almost 8.) Athanase finally died a few days later when they sliced through his mouth, deep enough to separate his bottom jaw.

I believe the Hutu killed him as a part of the violence incited by RTLM. The Hutu were trying to eliminate the Tutsi race. The Hutu hated the Tutsi because they said Tutsi were very intelligent and owned most of the cows (a measure of riches). The Tutsi had a lot of land and the Hutu resented them for it. The highest levels of the government taught the Hutu that if they kill the Tutsi, they would get the Tutsi's stuff and gain power. I think this is why the Hutu Interahamwe tortured and killed my uncle.

My auntie, Agnes, and her husband, Cyprian, were wounded and had to hide by the school as well. They found a house that had belonged to one of the killers, who had moved out and joined the other killers at the camp, and stayed in that house. The day when we moved to the bamboo bush was probably the only day we did not suffer a lot because when we left, the killers came and killed any who were left at the school. My aunt Agnes and her husband were also killed in the house they had moved to, and when we went back to check on them that night, we buried them. Burying was not as it used to be. A small hole was always enough to bury someone. Any wild animal could easily dig and get them out. Hoes were easily available and what we used to dig the holes for burial.

The day after we buried my aunt and her husband was the day Eric's father died. That night we went to the bamboo bush as usual because this was our place to stay. Many of us were always looking for food on the ground, in the gardens. One day, as we were searching for food, we were attacked.

Before the fighting began, my father sent me clothes for school and for special occasions. These clothes were very special to me, so when the fighting began and we fled from our house, I did not want to leave my clothes behind. I was determined to take them all with me, so

I put on all my pants, and then put my shorts on over them. I put on all my shirts and then put my t-shirts on over them. I looked very strange, with all these clothes. I looked like something from a Disney movie or a robot, but I was happy that I was able to take them all with me.

As we were being attacked, our plan was to climb to the top of the hill, which was called Kimpiri, and gather rocks and stones to throw down at the killers below. We did not think that they had guns and grenades and would be able to attack us easier than we could them. We started climbing and throwing rocks, which made the attackers angry. As they were coming up the hill, we saw them killing people who were in their way. They used machetes and sticks. As they got closer to us, they threw a grenade, and everyone in my group scattered. I do not remember how I was able to do it, but I found myself rolling down the hill and I ended up on the hillside at the bamboo patch. Many bodies were scattered on the hill, and on the hill was the filth from where people went to the bathroom in the open. I rolled through that filth and my beloved clothes were dirty. I noticed that my clothes stank, and I smelled myself and I smelled bad as well. I was disappointed that my clothes were dirty. It seems strange to me now to think that I was worried about my clothes in the middle of all the danger and killing, but as a child the clothes were important to me.

When I stopped rolling, I found myself beside my uncle Eugene's wife, Mukanyarwaya. We were at the bamboo patch, and we started making our way through the bamboo. The soldiers were shooting at us, and my aunt was hit in the foot. The shot tore the back of her heel off her foot, and she could not walk. She cried out to me to help her, but I did not feel I could save her, so I took off through the bamboo reeds. I was running from the killers and I came upon a woman I knew who was so terrified by the bullets she could not run. She asked me to bury her in the roots of the bamboo and cover her with leaves. At first I did not want to do this because I was afraid that I would kill her, but she begged me to do this, so I covered her up and jumped up and down to smooth the ground. I know burying her this way worked because she is still alive and has a family now! Then, I began running again. However, as I started moving, my pants started falling down around me. First, some of the shorts fell to my ankles. Then, some of them fell to my knees. Then, the pants started sliding from my waist. I could not run. While my pants were falling down, I was attacked by ants. They crawled on my legs, and bit me on my arms. They were biting me everywhere. As I was struggling to get the ants off, I thought, "I must commit suicide right now." During this time, many people used the river that ran through the bamboo bush to kill themselves. I decided that I would find the river and jump in and kill myself, so I started running to look for the river. I knew that it ran through the bamboo patch because I had seen it from the top of the hill. I went this way, and it wasn't there. I went that way, and it wasn't there. I went another way, and it wasn't there. No matter which way I went, I could not find the river. While I could not find the river and while I was struggling to get rid of the ants, I managed to get rid of some of the clothes. Losing some of the clothes made me relax and then I moved forward and ended up at a location in the bamboo bush where we camped before. None of the killers knew about this location. It happened to also be the end of the day. The government helicopter came over and the killing was over for the day. Because I could not find the water, and my clothes came off, and it was time for the killers to leave, the thoughts of suicide went away. I think all of this was God's way of protecting me.

I do not know how many miles I ran that day. I know I ran a long time and I was very exhausted. It is very interesting how God does things. I never got sick during all of this time, even though I was sleeping outside, did not have enough to eat, and was running so much. Now, I live in a house, have plenty to eat and no worries, and sometimes I get sick.

At this point, we decided to leave the school completely and hide only in the bamboo bush. The bamboo bush was our place to hide, but we did not sleep there during the night. During the night, we came out at 5 p.m. and camped at the edge of the bush. Some people camped at the edge of the bush and some moved to the houses near the bush. Some of the houses belonged to some of the people who were hiding. One of them, Rusatira, was famous to us because his house was large enough for many of us to sleep there at night. We used that house for many days because there were not so many mosquitoes in it, even though it was at the edge of the bush, which is why we tried to get as many as possible in that house. I remember one night we were sleeping at that house and our beds were the leaves of the banana tree. We put a bunch of leaves to dry and then put them together to make a bed. This was very normal for those of us who had cows because when you took cows to the pasture for many days, you used these banana leaves as a bed. As we were sleeping, one person on top of the other, someone came in and tried to light a match to see his way, but the match caught the leaves on fire. The whole house caught on fire. Some people woke up and screamed, and others were still sleeping. Some came out burned, and that is when I decided that I would not go back there to hide again. However, many people kept going back there to sleep. In fact, that is where we took people who were wounded on a daily basis. We moved them there to sleep and then back to the bamboo bush to hide during the day.

Every time we hid there was so much fear. Instead of having fear and running away with us, my cousin Simba moved forward toward the killers. He had a sword for his protection. He snuck behind them and went where they came from. Most of the time when he came back, he brought food because he could sneak behind the killers and get food at the same time. For this reason, he was a hero to many of us. While the killers were gone, we came out of the bamboo bush hungry and during that time, he was there with food. We were always surprised by his heart and his kindness because if he had not been there with food, we would have to go out of the bamboo bush and search for food. Simba did this throughout the genocide, from the first day until the day he was attacked and wounded, which resulted in his death.

As usual, by 9 a.m., we were ready to run back into the bamboo bush. The bush was under a big hill, and as the killers came they came with drums. They beat the drums and brought barking dogs and singing women. Once they got on top of the hill, we could see them very well. Some among us were still resistant and willing to fight against them. They grabbed arrows and swords, ready to fight. There were few of us able to fight because at this time we were weak enough. However, we still had the gun we got from the sniper. The guy who had the gun always tried to hide as far from us as he could, because they were looking for him. When we saw them on the hill, we immediately ran away through the bamboo bush. I remember that, at the beginning, the bamboo bush was very thick and concentrated, and you could hardly find a place to step. While you were running inside the bush, you saw people trying to hide at the very edge of the bamboo bush. One of those was my first grade teacher, and I said, "Are you sure they won't catch you?" He said, "No, I don't think they will find me." However, he died. We ran away and when I came out of the bush, his body was right there where he tried to hide. His name was Rugerinyange, and he was the first teacher I had in school. That day so many people died. You walked three feet, and there was a dead body. Four feet, and a body. Everywhere there were bodies. You just jumped over them. If it was someone you knew, you tried to cover them up with your extra clothes.

At that time, many of my family were still alive. Those who survived from the church and the school were still alive. My uncle Athanase's wife, Dorothea, had a tumor on her foot and could not move, so she always stayed at the edge of the bamboo bush, and somehow survived. My aunt Mukanyarwaya, who was shot in the heel, also survived. My uncle Eugene had a house boy, who was a Hutu, and he was there with us. He had malaria. Those three slept at the same place, and somehow they all managed to survive. Perhaps they were not killed because of the house boy. Not all of the Hutu turned against their employers.

When we came out from the bush, some people tried to find food in the gardens. The next day we woke up and got ready to run away. If you had one banana or one potato, you put it in your pocket and ran away with it. If you were wounded, you stayed there at the edge of the bamboo bush, as my family did. Many times when we came back, we found the wounded had died. One sad day was the day my cousin Runyonga was attacked and beaten in the head. When I came out, I saw her bleeding. I could not talk to her because she could not talk. We had to leave her and it was a very tough time. We made it through the day. As I camped, one of my relatives was already affected. The next day, we moved into the bush. I was hiding along with my cousin Rukara. He was younger than I was. We moved and were running away. I had a small machete in my hand, and as we were running inside the bush, we got trapped in a thick bush. We heard the killers behind us. They were screaming and we heard the dogs. My cousin started crying, and I thought, "What am I going to do?" I started cutting my way and was able to cut my way out. As we moved forward, I met my cousin Eric. As we got to the front, we were attacked again. As we were moving, the killers cut Eric's leg. The person who cut his leg was his neighbor. Eric called his name, and said, "Calixte, you cut me!" We pulled him out and ran away. Finally, we made it through the day. After that, Eric joined the others of my relatives who stayed at the edge of the bush because he could not move anymore. His leg got infected and was full of maggots.

The next day, we were hiding in the bamboo bush and I was moving with my cousin. Many people died there. I remember that my teacher's body was still there. I walked about three feet and I met a woman who lost her husband. She stopped me and said, "Stop, stop, I have a question. My husband was killed, and he had money in his pants cuffs. I am afraid of touching him, but I need his money. Maybe because you are a man, you can get it out." My cousin and I told her to show us where he was. His neck was cut and he was lying there. She pointed to his pants leg, and said, "The money is there." I remember getting the money out of his pants cuff, and she said, "Maybe when the war is over I can buy something to eat." I remember thinking, "At least you are hoping the war will be over." That day was over, and after that things got really, really crazy.

Things got crazy because the guy who had the gun we got from the sniper shot it in the air. The news went everywhere that the RPF was there with us. The government got really mad and decided they would send as much force as needed to kill us as soon as possible. The killers came at us with all they could. After they left, the bamboo bush looked like a normal street, because they cut down all the bamboo. So many people died. I remember seeing one of my neighbors, who was beaten in the head, and her brain was hanging out her head. Somehow, she survived and is normal today. As I came out of the bush, people I had passed by and were still alive were now dead. I remember getting to where I left my mat when I was running, and seeing that woman with her brain out. I was shocked. She was our neighbor – and she was my grandmother's daughter through baptism. I could not cry and she could not cry – it was just as if this was normal. They never found the man with the gun, and we moved out again. I was amazed to find that all of my relatives who were sleeping outside the bamboo bush were still alive.

The next morning, before we ran, some of our guys got food from the garden. As they were getting food, they met an old lady, who was a Hutu. Because of the madness and anger, they brought her to our camp and I remember them forcing her to bury all the dead bodies that were outside. Among those killed was a woman who had twins. One of the twins was killed, but the other was still alive and crawling on her mother. That child later died, also. I do not know what happened to the Hutu woman. After that, as usual, we ran away.

That day, it happened that the killers found my cousin Simba. As usual, he wanted to go behind where they had been. He fought because he had no other choice. There were many of them and only one of him. They finally got him down. However, he wounded two of them. They messed him up very badly. They cut his neck, his head, his arms and his legs and left him to die.

As my cousin Runyonga and I were hiding, the killers ran into her and told her she had to give them money. She knew I had money that I got from my grandmother. When she was attacked, she called my name and said, "Serge, Serge bring that money." The killers said, "Bring that money very quickly or we will kill her." In my mind I thought, "If I come out, they will kill me." In my heart, I was going to come out. As I was coming out, they cut her neck and I heard her screaming. She screamed, and I thought, "If I come out they will kill both of us, so there is no reason for me to come out, since they are already killing her." So I continued hiding. They did not see me and finally I heard the gun go off and I knew they would leave. In a few minutes, the helicopter was making the rounds.

As I was coming out, I was talking and my cousin Simba heard my voice. He called my name and I could tell immediately that was not good news. I could tell his voice was weak. I looked for him and found him lying in the mud. As soon as I saw him, I started crying and thinking that this was the end of the line. He was the person who brought food for us and the inspiration for us all. He was everything to me. As I got close to him, he said, "Serge, be strong." I think that this is some of what has made me who I am. I approached him and as I looked, I could see inside of his body. The bleeding was over and water was going through his body. He made conversation with me. I remember that I sat down and my crying stopped. He said, "Don't cry, because you will make me cry." I thought that talking to him was support I could give him during that moment. I talked to him and I remember we talked about how we should always be strong when things happened to us. He told me how he deserved to go to heaven. He told me to just be mature and not to worry about him; I should just worry about my future. As soon as he said that, I cried to death. It was getting dark and I thought, "I need to go out and go get my uncle Eugene so he can come and help me get him out," because I was not strong enough to get him out alone. I told my uncle, "Hey, let's go get my brother, he is wounded." My uncle was traumatized already and he just kept saying we would get someone to help us. That night, Simba was in the bush with many dead bodies. In the morning, very early, my first thought was to go see how he was doing. When I got there, he was very hungry and his body was covered with goose bumps. I was angry that I could not help to get him out. He was cut into pieces and there was no way you could lift pieces, so the only way to help was to bring food to him. That day we were not attacked, and I ran around asking for food. The RPF began weakening the killers, so we were more comfortable moving about out of the bush during the daytime. Before that, there was no choice to be on the outside – you either went into the bamboo bush or you were killed. I managed to find a family of four that had four potatoes. I asked if they had any food that I could give to my brother. They said "no" and then they said, "Tell us what happened to your brother." I sat down and told them what had happened and finally they said, "Here is one potato." I took the potato to Simba. He was able to eat the potato after one day without eating. Because of this story of getting food for my brother, I feel that I will always speak for the weak people, the sick and the orphans. I think this is also the drive that made me start my foundation.

After this, we started hearing a lot of gun noise because the RPF was getting closer and closer to winning the battle against the killers. We were very excited because we thought that we were going to be saved. At that time, the attacks on us slowed down and we started thinking that the killers were losing and that they were looking for a way to escape themselves.

The next step for us was finding a way to bury the bodies that were around us. We relaxed for about two days, during which time there were very few attacks on us. At that time, I thought my life was beginning to change for the better. I had some money that my grand-mother gave me, and I used some of it to buy 20 sweet potatoes and I kept those sweet potatoes for about a week. I used those sweet potatoes to feed my cousin Simba. The potatoes were already cooked, and imagine having 20 cooked sweet potatoes, and no refrigerator to put them in. By the end of the week, they smelled really bad. By that time, Simba was outside of the bamboo bush, where he was living for a few days. Every day we ran around the camp trying to make sure nobody who was hurt was not being taken care of.

RESCUE

The RPF (composed of refugees who had fled to Uganda and other countries) gained control of Rwanda on July 4, 1994. It was a moment of relief for many of us. During the genocide, the Hutu took the cattle owned by the Tutsi for themselves. If you had a herd of 200 cows before, you might be left with 10 cows after the genocide. The Hutu could not keep the property, because the RPF came in after the genocide and restored the rights to the citizens. However, the Hutu did take personal belongings and destroyed homes by taking off the roofs or destroying entire buildings.

When the RPF got into our district, Nyamata, it was a scary time again because we started hearing heavy weapons. We still had that gun we got from the sniper, but we were scared to death. The first thing the RPF did when they got to our district was send a person from our area, who joined them. They sent him to tell us to come out of the bamboo bush and go to the District of

Nyamata. The first thing he did was come and pass by his parents' home. When he got to his home, he found his mother, who had been sleeping on a bed since the genocide started and was still alive. I do not know how she survived, but I remember the man telling us that when he saw his mother he said, "Mom, I know you are hurting and I miss you, but the one way I can save the people in the bamboo bush is to use you." He said, "Mom, I want you to go to the bamboo bush and tell them that the RPF is here and you should come out as soon as possible." He did this because he knew if he came, some people might get scared and he might be attacked. His mother came, crawling through the streets, and she managed to get to the hill above the bamboo bush. I remember we saw her waving, and she could not talk at all. Some of us managed to reach her, and some decided to approach her and see if she was one of the killers. Once they approached her, she told them, "My son, who joined the RPF, has just come and he wants you to move to the headquarters of Nyamata." We were very suspicious of her because we did not know her and we thought it might be a trap, a way the killers were using to finish everyone who was left. Suddenly, one of the men in the group recognized her and that is when he said, "She is a Tutsi, and she would not lie to us." After that we were very excited, and we began jumping around, saying that, "We are going to be saved." As a kid, I did not think twice and immediately joined the people up front who were moving toward the RPF. I left my relatives, who were lying on the ground near the bamboo bush, and ran to the city. As we were about to get to Nyamata, we were in a big line and we were all so excited. We carried with us all the small weapons we had and I remember I had my small machete. As we got to a narrow street that had a tree on the side, we heard a voice that said, "Drop your weapons and move forward." I remember a guy in our group, who we used to call "Captain," refused to drop his weapon and the guy in the tree, who was a RPF soldier, said, "Please drop your weapons or the killers will capture you again." Captain kept refusing and refusing, but the RPF guy was able to hunt him down and tie him up with a rope, and the rest of us moved into the city. When we got to the city, it was like being on our way to heaven. We met RPF people who were such an encouragement and emotional support to us. They told us, "You have been saved," and "We will provide everything," and encouraged those of us who could to join them for the next battle because there was still fighting in other cities.

Once I reached the city and saw how things were going to be better for us, I immediately decided to go back to the bamboo bush that evening to get the rest of my relatives out. On my way out, I was stepping over dead bodies, jumping over them. The road was smelly, flies were everywhere. I remember passing by skeletons that were smiling. I managed to reach the bamboo bush. As soon as I got there, I met some of the RPF family who were there already. They were talking to the wounded, trying to encourage them to be strong. Immediately, my cousin Simba passed away. It was Simba's dream to one day see the RPF army who fought for freedom and tried to rescue him. Putting myself in his position, I cannot think of anything he appreciated more than seeing those guys who had risked their lives and were coming to save him, even though it was too late for them to save his life. My cousin Runyonga had passed away also. The next thing was to bury them. We buried them at the bamboo bush and, as a family, we gathered those who were still alive – the group who was sleeping outside the bamboo bush, and who, by God's grace, were never captured by the killers. We moved them to the city, and when we got there the RPF had put in place people to take care of the wounded and sick. We put them in the school that was converted to a hospital. My cousin Bosco, my uncle Eugene's son, and I decided to go inside the city to find things to eat, as many were doing. Many people broke into stores. My cousin went his way and I went my way – he went one direction, I went another direction. I happened to meet a guy and we decided to break into a store and get some food out. This was a normal behavior during any war. That guy was really big, so he said, "Serge, why don't you go through this small hole and try to get inside and then open the door for me?" I went through a window and got in, and once inside I was able to open another window that was larger and this guy joined me inside. It was very dark and we could not see anything. This guy found a match and used it to see things. As he was trying to find things, I ran into a package of candies. I got so busy eating the candy that I forgot to get other things out. As this guy was searching things, he mistakenly lit a can of gasoline on fire. Immediately, there were flames. I dropped the candy and started trying to find my way out. The building filled with smoke and my eyes were stinging. I finally found a window that I could get out, but the guy could not get out and the store burned with him inside. After that, I said that I would never break into a store again.

We probably spent about three days going through stores looking for food and clothes. The RPF was not happy for us to do this, and told us not to because they would provide for us. However, we were out of control and did not listen. We slept outside at a soccer field. Outside in the city was like a bedroom – you saw people sleeping here, other people sleeping here, other people sleeping here, and that was normal. The RPF tried to get blankets for those of us sleeping outside.

Serge Gasore standing in the location of his home prior to the genocide. The spot he is standing on is where his bedroom was located. His home was destroyed by the Interahamwe.

Serge Gasore standing under the tree where he slept many nights during the time he was hiding from the killers during the genocide.

Serge Gasore standing by the slab of rock that was his bed many nights and days while in hiding from the killers during the genocide.

Serge Gasore kneeling in front of the skulls and bones of his friends, neighbors and family who were killed in the attack on the Catholic Church at Ntarama. This is the church where he sought refuge with his grandmother. She was among those killed in this attack.

MOVING FORWARD AFTER THE GENOCIDE

My uncle Eugene started as a volunteer cooking at the hospital (school) where the sick and wounded were taken. Then he got a position as head of the kitchen, and when he got that job he was able to move all of us to his compound. As a result of my uncle's job, he was able to move his wife to the hospital. She was the one who was shot in the heel. I also received treatment for the wounds I received when I was beaten on the head and cut on my leg with the machete. My cousin Eric was also moved to the hospital, along with his mother, and got treatment for the machete cut to his leg.

Many other things changed for us during this time. We stayed with people we did not know. We had plenty to eat. As a result of going so long without food, when food became available I ate everything that was around. At first, I had stomach problems from this. I was full and I could not breathe, and the gas backed up in my throat. I could not sleep and I was up the whole night. After one night like this, I did not eat so much the next day.

Our life was getting much better, but so many things were still going on. All those people who survived the genocide were attacked by many diseases. They ate unsafe foods, the city was dirty and many went to the hospital because of cholera and other diseases. At that time, all of my relatives contracted cholera and whoever was not sick was wounded and lying in the hospital bed. My cousin Bosco and I took care of them because most of the time we were healthy, and my other cousins were very young and unable to do anything. My uncle was taking care of his wife and my cousin Bosco also contracted cholera. After that, our life became miserable because we were confused. The person who was taking care of us, my uncle Eugene, was sick. We wondered how we would survive. My uncle Eugene's house boy, who was the Hutu who stayed with us in the bamboo, was also sick with malaria. After a while he got better and was my uncle's right hand. He took care of us, and I remember he was also able to rescue some cows. After the genocide, some cows were roaming around and we found some that belonged to us. During that time, the house boy decided to go steal some cows just because he was in love with cows. He got caught and was prosecuted and we never saw him again. He was good to us and we really missed him after that.

About that same time, our neighbor Celestin, who was a Hutu, came to Nyamata. He tried to sneak in, and I think he came because he thought he would be forgiven. However, it was too late for him. As soon as he came into the city, he met another guy who knew him and who was involved in the killing. He immediately took Celestin to a group and accused him of being one of the killers. I really liked Celestin, but by the time I heard about him being there, it was too late – he had already been killed. People were very angry and vengeance was something no one thought twice about.

We kept living there, but many people who were my friends and neighbors were dying every day because of the cholera. I could not help anymore and I was burying at least three people every day who were my friends or my classmates. It was so sad. I decided that the one way I could survive was to join the RPF. If I died, maybe I would die by a bullet instead of dying by cholera. I went to a house by the street where the members of the RPF stopped for food and gasoline, and rested if they needed to. I told the lady there to tell any soldiers that came by I was interested in joining them. She told me that she would. It was not long before she came to me at 3 a.m. and screamed in the window. She said, "Serge, I found people to take you." I was very excited. I did not think about this twice and I immediately went out. I was sleeping by my cousin Bosco and he never knew where I went. I did not tell any of my family I was leaving – I just disappeared.

When I got to the RPF, they gave me tea to drink. They had drinks and were talking and around 10 a.m. we took off. We went to Kigali, which was very close, but because of the war we took back roads to get there. On our way, a lot of Hutu roadblocks were in the street. Many times those roadblocks were abandoned, but there were trees across the road and the road was closed. Many times when we got to the roadblocks, we stopped far away and the soldiers who were with me went and surrounded the roadblocks to be sure they were safe. Roadblocks were also our occasion to catch chickens in the field, and goats as well. After the soldiers made sure the roadblock was not a trick, we ran into the field and chased chickens. This was also fun for us, because it was a long trip and this was a time to relax. We did this over and over again until we reached another province of my country called Kibungo. I remember once, after we got into the city, we had a big pot of rice cooked with about 10 cans of tomato paste. I cannot tell you why we used 10 cans of tomato paste – it was probably because we were hungry for such a long time and we wanted to eat as much as possible, especially those things we had not had in such a long time. I remember drinking a cup of tea and putting in so much sugar that half the cup was sugar. We had not had sugar in a long time and sugar was something we got for free. We ate chicken that was cooked in oil. We were ravenous, and so we ate as much as we possibly could.

After this, we continued our trip and ended up in Kigali. This was my first time to see the city, except for the time I was there at a very young age, so I did not know what the city looked like. When we got there, they made me take a shower. This was my first shower in 100 days and I cannot tell you how the water was. The water felt like a knife to me. I had to throw away my clothes that my father sent me. They were crawling with lice. I remember opening the cuffs on my shorts and the lice were just crawling around. You could grab handfuls of them and throw them into the air. I became accustomed to them, so they were not even bothering me. I was given new clothes to wear. After that, I went to bed. However, going to bed there was not fun at all because bullets were flying through the air. The RPF was still fighting with the soldiers who were left of the killers.

In the morning, I woke up and there I was in Kigali. I received some training – some defense training, such as how to use a gun and how to shoot. That was basically all the training I received until I joined the operation crew that was based in the north part of my country. That is when I received more training.

After a few nights in Kigali, my boss, who was an RPF Lieutenant, was sent to the north part of Rwanda. When he moved there, he left me in the capital city. At that time, I stayed with my co-worker. We stayed in a huge house that was captured by the RPF. It had a lot of things inside. At that time, no one else but soldiers were in the area of Kigali known as Remera – an area where there was a lot of fighting between the RPF and the former government. People had fled, so no civilians were left, and usually my daily duty was to watch the house. During the day, one thing I did was go inside the houses where no one was living and pick up anything that was useful, because the houses were abandoned. In those houses, many things happened to me. I remember that one day I went to a house that was owned by a former government official, a very strong government supporter who was very rich. The house was so big and was locked up. Immediately, when I saw the house, I told myself that I had to get into the house and get the stuff out. I remember that inside the house there happened to be dogs. I climbed the gate and got inside the house. Once I got inside the house, I started looking inside the bedrooms and closets, getting everything that I could take with me. I got everything and put it by the gate and was ready to break the gate and come out with the stuff. I was excited that I was surrounded by free and good stuff. In my perspective, getting into that house was like getting into heaven. I had not been in the capital city in a long time, and suddenly I was in a big city full of stuff. The gate was very tall, and I was trying to figure out how I was going to get out, and I was struggling with how I would get out. I grabbed a stone and started beating on the lock, trying to break it. As I was beating on the lock, a dog that was left inside the house heard me. He had not heard me before, but when he heard me that moment was miserable. The dog was bigger than I and he started barking. He was approaching me and I wasn't sure what to do. I had a grenade, but I did not want to use it because that would make the situation worse. I ran and ran and got back inside the house and the dog lost me. He went back inside his cage, and then I came back out. I decided that rather than trying to break the gate I would go back over the fence the way I came in. I started throwing things over the gate – clocks, small things from the house, and such. I think I was being stupid because when I went over the wall to come out, everything I had thrown over the gate was broken. I was very scared then to go back into people's houses.

I went into a house a second time and there was a person who was murdered inside the house, lying on a mattress. A dog was in the house, eating on the person who was killed. The dog jumped at me, and I ran away. As I ran, with the dog chasing me, a group of soldiers in the area shot the dog. Since that time I have had a fear of dogs – especially if they do not have an owner. By that time, dogs had eaten so many people it was easy for them to go after people who were alive.

I kept going into houses for about a month. Then one night, my boss told the truck driver, who usually came into Kigali to get new soldiers, to pass by the house and pick me up. I was sitting there with my co-worker and as I was sitting there, they came to me and said, "Hey, you need to pack up your stuff and let's go." I was angry that all my stuff was gone and I would be leaving everything that I got from other people's houses. We left and drove through the whole night. The little stuff that I had with me was in the back where the other soldiers were sitting. When we got to where we were going, I looked for my stuff and it was nowhere to be found. However, this was not a time to be looking for your stuff, and so I got there with only the clothes that I had. My boss was very happy to see me again and I lived in the area for a long time – probably more than four months.

While I was living with my boss, my job was to be an overnight guard while my crew was in operations. Our job was to make sure the area was safe. We were to make sure no killers were left in the area and to bring those we found to justice. I remember during that time while I was living with my boss, I found a pack of cigarettes on the bed and I smoked half of the pack at one time. I got very confused, threw up and had a terrible headache, and could not stand up. My boss asked me what happened to me and I told him nothing, that I had just a headache. He immediately took me to a military hospital. This hospital was in a nearby church where so many people were killed. I stayed in that hospital for a week, but they could not figure out what was going on with me, and I never told them because I thought they would think I was crazy.

After I was released from the hospital, I moved back to our headquarters. At the headquarters, life started to become normal. My normal job was standing by the roadblocks in the street. I remember one day, my cousin Claude, my uncle Anthase's son, happened to drive down the highway where I worked the roadblock. He was in a different location during the genocide, so neither of us knew if the other was alive until this time. He was surprised to see me at the roadblock. My responsibility was maintaining toughness and staying calm, so I could not greet him with as much emotion as I felt. I asked him for his travel documents and he cleared to pass through the roadblock. As soon as he got to Kigali, Claude told my uncle Antoine, who joined the RPF from Congo where he was in school, that I was alive. Antoine was my uncle who cared so much about me and that cheered him a little bit because he always wanted me to be with the family.

About that time, I learned about a man named Gatete, a Hutu and a leader in Kiramuruzi district. During the genocide he dug a hole so deep that just falling in it would kill you. He had the Tutsi taken to that hole and pushed in, and that hole took so many people's lives. I cannot tell you how many people were killed by this man. Beside the hole was a house. Gatete forced people into the house and then caved the house in on top of them, killing them. Some of my friends, who were soldiers, took me to see this place and many dogs surrounded the area. The dogs welcomed us with much barking and attacked us as we approached. As soon as the dogs attacked us, my friends told me the only way to avoid them was to shoot them and have them run away. I visited the hole and never forgot the sight. I tried to look in, but you could not see the bottom of the hole. I could not imagine how Gatete dug the hole. So many people died you would expect it to be full and you could not even see the bottom of it.

I was staying at the headquarters, but it wasn't long before we returned to Kigali. By the time we got into Kigali, the government started settling everything. It was time for school to start and the government structure was beginning to be back in place. Because of this, my boss decided that I should go to school while I was still in the RPF. He got me one morning and got me some books, and took me to school. I kept going to school and doing some work for the RPF. I did whatever they asked me to do – overnight guarding or whatever. One day, my boss, who was in charge of the RPF property, was assigned to another area called Gashora where RPF agriculture was. Before we left, we stopped by Nyamata center, where he had a meeting with other RPF leaders. I had a gun called a SMG, and I sat with a number of soldiers. As I sat with my friends, I played with the safety on the gun. Another soldier watched me, but he did not say anything to me. I played with the gun like it was a guitar. Once I stopped playing with the safety, the gun was in shooting position. The soldier immediately came and tackled me, and when he grabbed me, he said, "Do you want to shoot someone?" I said, "How?" and he said the safety was off. He grabbed the gun and me and took me to the boss and told him that, "Serge was trying to shoot someone." I do not know why he did this, whether he really suspected me of being a killer or whether he was trying to get me in trouble. Immediately his boss, the mayor, took my gun and jumped into his car along with his bodyguard. They told my boss and me that we had to follow them. My heart was beating because I was not wearing full uniform and my gun was open, so I did not know what to expect from my boss. However, we had to go because his boss outranked my boss. We moved from Nyamata to an RPF base called Gato. As soon as we got to Gato, the mayor turned and went back to where we came from. All that time we were following him. Once we got to Nyamata, he turned around and told us to follow him again. We kept following him and then, at 6 p.m., they gave my gun back to my boss, but told him they were keeping me there. We went back to Gato and I was taken to jail. There, I was with other soldiers who had also committed stupid mistakes. However, I had the sympathy of other soldiers in the barracks. A group of senior officers wanted to talk to me. I guess it was because I was very young and very obedient. Instead of taking me to a jail cell, one of the captains told them he would keep me. For about two nights, I stayed outside the jail, sleeping on a car seat that was just put on the ground between some trees. I think they forgot about me, but then someone saw me and told me that my boss was looking for me. When he left me, he went ahead and finished his mission, and then came back to find me. We went back to Kigali and I stayed with him and went to school. It was no secret that he cared about me because he tried to protect me from the dangerous missions and saw to it that I went to school.

After my cousin told my uncle about seeing me, we moved back to Kigali. While walking through the streets there, I ran into another cousin, Bobe, who had come there. He was going to get water and I saw him. I took him with me to the headquarters and from then on he knew where I was. I think he passed this information on to my uncle Antoine. While I was living with my boss, I received a couple of visits from my cousin Diane, who survived the killing in the church.

My uncle Antoine wanted me to get my education through the family instead of through the RPF. The difference was that instead of serving in the RPF and having duties after my school day was over, I would go home to family and live with them.

I remember waking up each morning about 5:30 a.m. at the headquarters and my uncle was at the door, knocking, and requesting to meet my boss. My boss kept denying him, but my uncle never gave up. It became normal for me to expect my uncle at the door when we opened in the morning. My boss could not just let me leave the RPF without getting permission from his boss. You had to have a reason to leave the RPF, even though it was not a rebel RPF and we did not have contracts. It was up to my boss and the RPF to let me leave. When my uncle came to ask him to let me go back to the family, he hesitated and then he finally approved it. It took about four months before my uncle finally got approval for me to leave.

My boss told me to get my things together and get ready to go home. By this time, many in my family had been killed, including my grandmother, and my family was scattered from our home village, so my boss knew that things could be difficult for me if I went home.

When I left the RPF, I went to my father's home in Kigali. When I got there, I was received into the family. I kept going to school, and then things began to get difficult. I was living in a new city and having to make new friends. I expected to have a life similar to what I knew before the genocide occurred, but this did not happen as I expected. I was not stable and unable to focus on school because of what I went through and also because of events that happened outside of school. In spite of this, I was able to able to keep up with my school work and progress each year to the next grade.

I remember when friends and neighbors were very kind to me during the many problems I went through, either in the class or outside the class. Many people lifted me up when times were tough and that stays in my heart and makes me want to also lift up other people who have downfalls in their life, or who seem to be weak.

During the time I lived with my family, I learned a lot of lessons about life – that life is not always perfect and even in peaceful times, life is not always easy. While I was in school, I saw people who had values different than mine. I was back in school and in the fourth grade. The teachers were my neighbors and a mixture of Tutsi and Hutu. I had a good relationship with my teachers. I remember that sometimes I was late to class, and I was punished like the other kids, but no longer because I was a Tutsi.

After about three years, when I was entering my first year of high school, I ended up leaving my family and went to live with a friend. I immediately entered high school and was able to go to school and work at the same time. While I was living with my friend, I managed to visit many of my relatives during vacations.

Life was not easy —I was still struggling with my past, struggling with where I was heading for the future. But God gave me the strength and energy and power to keep going, because I wanted to be a courageous person and not be discouraged by what was going on around me. I have told and will continue to tell people who get discouraged by small things to seek strength and power from God because He is in control of what we do.

During the time I was living with my friend, my uncle Antoine was able to leave the RPF legally and was able to get his own house. He also became the mayor of a district. I was in touch with him and he knew what was going on in my life, and he thought it was in my best interest to go and live with him in Ngenda. He was newly married at this time. When I got to my uncle's house, things changed tremendously because he and his wife cared about me and wanted to restore my life.

This is when I began having the life a normal kid would expect to have. Because of this, my grades in class changed tremendously. I became emotionally stable and started becoming a leader among my peers. My peers began seeing good in me. I started reflecting about things and I began to dream again. I dreamed about a future. The key to all these things changing in my life was the fact that my uncle and his wife were very supportive of me – whether I was wrong or right, they were always supportive. If I did something wrong, they had a good way to correct it or mention it without chastising me or accusing me. This opened my eyes because they gave me a freedom I never had before and I came to realize that freedom was what I was missing that would allow me to perform like other kids.

My uncle's wife was a professor at the high school I attended. She had a degree in chemistry and I was also a chemistry major in high school. I remember going to her and asking for help with my biology. She just put biology in my head and I went to class breathing biology and chemistry. Because she was always open to my requests for help, I always wanted to perform my best. Her father was a history teacher at my school, and I remember making 10 out of 10 in his class, and he was overwhelmed because I was the only person to get 10 out of 10 in his class. Even now, whenever I talk to him, he talks about that. After one year teaching me at the high school, my aunt moved to Kigali to pursue her degree at the Kigali Institute of Education. She lived in a boarding school there and sometimes came home on weekends or during vacation times.

At this time in high school, I started exploring the talents I had. I became a comedian and I started playing soccer, basketball and doing karate. At the school, the headmaster got to know me because of the famous comedy I performed during the school-year opening ceremony. I made up a story about Russia and Chechnya. This story told how the Russian troops were in a parade, singing and excited about fighting Chechnya and winning. The funny thing about this was that when this army was in the parade, their guns were plates and forks. The plates and forks were metal, so every time we knocked on a plate, it made a sound and the people went crazy. After this comedy, I became famous at my high school. I had not yet thought about becoming a runner, but I was always excited about seeing people run.

The headmaster realized that I was a good leader and one day he showed up in our class because our class was making noise. Our class did not have a chief – although each class had a chief. The chief that we had was not well-respected by his peers, and the headmaster decided he should leave and I took over. I became a good class leader and my classmates always appreciated that I never became rude or mean to them.

By that time, my uncle lived near the school and I took some of my classmates to my uncle's home, and I gave them food and milk because they were away from their parents. I had a good relationship with my classmates. During high school I had a best friend named Olivier, and we are still good friends even now. I am always thankful that long distance has not broken our relationship. During vacation I took time to visit with him.

My uncle and aunt taught me most of the good character that I have now. Being comfortable in my uncle's house helped me study well for the national exam that ends high school. I finished it with good grades. At the same time, I was running, striving to get better and hoping to get a scholarship overseas.

While I was living with my uncle, we had a great time. My uncle was a great man, very well-respected. I lived in a boarding school, which was very near the house, during the school year and then went to my uncle's house during vacations. There were times during the school year that I went home so I could concentrate more on my studies. When I went to his house I chose to sleep in a different house from where my uncle stayed. He had two houses in a compound. In one house, two of my cousins, a house boy and I lived. My uncle and his wife, my cousin Faina, and another woman, who worked for the district, lived in the other house. I used the house boy's room as a study room and to be even more independent. In this house, my cousin Gakuba also stayed in a different room. I had a room in my uncle's house, also. One day I did not have a lot to study, so I decided to stay in my room in my uncle's house. That day I was hanging out with my cousin Faina. We hung out until about 10 p.m. and at exactly 10 p.m., I told him I was going to bed. My uncle and his wife were already asleep. As soon as I got to bed, I heard Gakuba knocking on the door to my uncle's house. He screamed, "The house boy is dead." I was confused and I flew from the bed. As soon as I got in the living room, everyone was in there and I saw that Gakuba was naked and coughing. He said, "I think the house boy is dead because somebody is burning the house." The district stored many mattresses at the house and they were in the room where I used to stay. We saw the house was burning, so immediately my uncle gave us flashlights and told us to go hunt whoever had done this. Gakuba and I grabbed the traditional weapons we had in our house and took off through the neighborhood, trying to find who had done this thing. It was very dark, and there were bushes so you could not see. We ran around and ran around, but we found no clue as to who set the fire. We went back to the compound when we realized there was no way to find the people, and when we got back home the neighbors had come and helped fight the fire. We went inside to check on the house boy and we found him dead. We asked Gakuba what happened, and he said he heard some people walking by and heard the window blasting and then he did not pay any attention and went back to sleep. Then, smoke came into his room and he smelled it but did not figure out what was going on. Finally, the smoke woke him up and he tried get out of the house, but the house boy had locked the door and hid the key and he could not find the key. You could see his fingerprints on the wall where he was searching for the key. He finally found the key and was able to get out of the house. When we went inside to check on the house boy, you could see where he struggled to find his way out. Afterwards, we buried the house boy. This event is still in my mind, and every time I smell smoke it reminds me of it. Even when I see smoke on television, I remember this fire. The thing that really stays with me about that night is that I was supposed to be with the house boy that night and I could have died that night. I feel guilty because I feel that somehow I could have helped him or suffered with him. He was a nice man and very humble; he was a Christian and so good to me. I think if I was there with him, maybe together we could have survived or I could have helped him.

There was an investigation, but there was no conclusion as to who did this. If the attackers were found, we were never told. It was so sad for that young man to lose his life in such a horrid way.

While I was living with my uncle, I was playing soccer, basketball and doing karate. I started thinking about what I was doing. Soccer is a very famous game in my country and in the whole continent of Africa in general. It is much like basketball or baseball in the United States. Children play the game in the street, and set up goals in the street and when they hear a car coming by they move the goals. With this in mind, I began to think, "I am good in soccer, but I am not the best. I am good in basketball, but I am not the best. I am good in karate, but I am not the best." So I thought that I should try something I had never done. I thought to myself that because I always ran to school or wherever I needed to go and did not get tired easily, why should I not pursue a running career? I joined a group of people from school who woke up in the mornings and went running. Then, one of the life principals at school made a rule that everyone had to run in the morning. I was happy about this rule and I decided that I would always do extra running to see what I could do. I began doing this, but I did not see fast improvement in my running, so I decided to stop and go back to playing soccer. I stopped running for a while.

While I was living with my uncle, my country held elections for a new president. Because my uncle Antoine was mayor, he had a lot of things to work on to make the election go smoothly. He had a lot to work on, and so he was not getting a lot of rest and enough sleep. One evening, he came in suffering a stomachache. He came in asking for me, but I wasn't there. He was suffering, and so they took him to the hospital. When I got home, I found they took him to the hospital, and I learned he was bleeding internally. I called my uncle Teogene, who lived in Kigali, to see if he could bring my uncle's wife, who was studying at the Kigali Institute of Education University, to be with him. Teogene immediately came that night and we stayed at the hospital all night until it was safe to move my uncle Antoine to Kigali, to a bigger hospital.

They left my cousin Faina and me to take care of the house. This happened during school vacation, and one day I was walking around and heard that there was a running competition. I knew that there was a guy who was practicing for the competition because I saw him running early in the morning. I decided that I would just go run and give it a try. I went the next morning to compete. I had no shoes for the race, as all my shoes were old dress shoes. I had no shorts for running, only jean shorts. I went with my jean shorts and barefooted. We were lined up to run a ten- kilometer (10K) road race and my heart was beating. The prize was 10,000 franc, which equaled about $16 (U.S.). I wanted that money so badly and as I looked around at the others, I saw the man I saw running every morning. I just thought, "I'll do my best."

As we did warm-ups, the guy I saw running began giving me advice. He told me, "Serge, when you are running don't try to use your arms a lot, because it can make you get tired." I thought, "Oh, I can relate to that." We kept doing warm-ups and then we were called for the race. The gun went off and we took off. We ran and ran and ran. That guy and I were up front running and running, up to the five-kilometer (5K) mark. After the 5K mark, the guy started breathing very funny and I thought, "I might beat you." I decided to take off with all my energy. I looked around and no one was around me. The guy was behind me, and there I was running barefoot and in my jean shorts. Everyone else had very good shoes and good shorts and looked professional, but I won the race and was given the 10,000 franc. As soon as I got the money in my hand, I called the hospital and talked to my uncle's wife. I said, "You know what? I won the running race and now I have 10,000 franc." I think I was being stupid enough to call and laugh when I knew that my uncle was suffering. I think they were very happy and proud of me, but we did not make a long conversation about it. My uncle was able to be released from the hospital and returned home. He was very proud of my running and was supportive of me.

A few weeks after that, as I was walking again, I got word that there was festival at a school. I saw people in line, jumping around, being excited and cheering. I asked what was going on and I was told there was a race about to happen. They said it was a 5K race and the winner got a training kit. I asked if just anyone could participate in the race and they said yes. I had on jeans, but I had some very, very short shorts with me, so I decided to just take off my jeans and got in line. The gun went off and I raced a few guys, who were very tough, but I won again. After that, I became popular in my area, but I never recognized that I was getting stronger and stronger in running. I did not stay active in running for a while and I started losing some of my running skills.

One day, there was a regional competition for school. A friend of mine named Jean-Marie, who won a lot of awards and national titles, made an announcement at a school assembly that the competition would be the next week and anyone who wanted to sign up was welcome to. Jean-Marie was captain of our school team. Here I was, Serge, who ran but never paid attention to running and said, "I'll sign up." Jean-Marie put me in the 5K race and he entered the 10K. We went to run at the province and I was the only one entered who did not seem professional. Everyone else had good shoes and good shorts and was ready to run —and there I was, with shoes that did not have a bottom. The bottoms of my shoes were almost off and I had borrowed them from a classmate. I told my classmate, "Let's run." By the 2.5K mark I made it around everyone, and at the end of the 5K I won. After this race, I told myself seriously that I was going to be a runner. I told myself the second and third time, "I am going to run my tail off."

We went back to school and I tried thinking what would come from my running if I focused on it. I said to myself that I was doing well in class and I knew that people ran for the national team, and they were recruited by schools or foreign countries to run for them. I thought, "Why not run and see if I could be recruited by the national team?" I also thought I could later use that opportunity to get a foreign scholarship or international recruitment.

In my country, when you pass the national exam and have good grades you get a Presidential Scholarship. While I was thinking about focusing on running, I also wanted the Presidential Scholarship. So, I decided to focus and see what would come from those two goals. I got up early in the morning and ran. I ran around the neighborhood and ran out in the countryside, and then came back to the school, and got water and took a shower and went to class.

As I was doing this – struggling to study and run and practice – the headmaster of the school heard that I was training hard to get ready for the next season, and that on weekends I ran from one city to another city, which was around 25 miles round-trip. He decided that he would support me by providing me with an energy drink. When he did that, I was very encouraged. You could tell that the captain for our team was worried that I would beat him. He came to the regional competition and gave out tickets for the national competition. He was known for running the 10K, but he left that race to enter the 1500-meter run. I entered the 5K and the 10K, and won both. By this time, I had shoes and shorts. They were not professional gear, but they were fine. In both races I made it around everyone and I was becoming famous in my district. Before I got home, my uncle knew that I won a race, but he did not know anything else about it. The headmaster was proud of me, and I was proud of myself.

The national exam for high school students, which every high school student in Rwanda has to take, was getting closer. I kept training. We did not have lights in our classroom, so we used petroleum lamps, but the petroleum was expensive. Without studying until 2 a.m. during this time you could never expect to pass the national exam. After class ended at 5 p.m., I trained for running until 6 p.m., took a shower, ate, and lit my lamp and got to studying. I did this the whole semester, and when the national exam came I passed and received a Presidential Scholarship. I was very excited and happy. I achieved my first goal. I was able to graduate from high school.

By winning a Presidential Scholarship, I was able to attend a public university for free. My father was very proud of my scholarship, but he felt that if I got an education in Germany it would help me have more influence in my country when I returned home. He had a friend in Germany who started working on getting me a scholarship there.

By the time results of the exam came out, my uncle had finished his term as mayor and moved to Kigali. This meant that I had to go and live with him in Kigali. I felt this would be a chance for me to show what I could do in running because professional runners were in Kigali and I thought if I connected with them and trained with them, I could become someone. Once in Kigali, I attended the University.

As soon as I got to Kigali, I found a group of military people, who I met at the national competitions I attended. They became my friends and we are still friends even now. We began training in the morning at 6 a.m., came home and did some homework, and then in the evening we hung out together if we did not train that day. Some days we trained. After a while, I entered a national competition. I ran the 10K, and during that competition I met a lot of professional runners because after I won the race everyone came to me and wanted me to run for their club. The national team was also interested in me. I kept competing and I could tell that I was approaching my second goal, which was to compete on the national level, but I wasn't there yet.

As I was running for the national team, a guy named Leopold, a professional runner who was well-connected to Abilene Christian University in the United States and now lives in Canada, approached me. He said, "Serge, I am very proud of your performance. You are smart in class, you are running fast and in America, a school called Abilene Christian University (ACU) could be a good fit for you." I could tell that God was opening doors for me. The fact that the word "Christian" appeared in the school's name made me think I could not believe what was just happening to me. I was very happy already that my dad was trying to find me a scholarship in Germany, but the possibility of going to the United States was icing on a cake. Without thinking about it even once, I said, "That would be great." After that, Leopold started working on trying to arrange things for me to go to ACU. A lot of paperwork is involved in being able to go to the U.S. – getting a visa issued and things like that. I received e-mails from the track coach at ACU. It was not long afterwards when I received a call from ACU asking me to join their track and field program.

Serge Gasore as a high school student.

COMING TO AMERICA

I attended the University, but now I had my visa and it was time for me to leave my home and family behind. Speaking very little English, I left the familiar surroundings of my home country and made my way to Abilene, Texas. It was in Abilene and at ACU that God allowed my faith to be restored in him.

The Ministry of Sports for Rwanda purchased a plane ticket for me to travel to the U.S. I boarded a plane in Rwanda and had no idea where I was going. I had my passport, my passport had my school name in it and said the school was in the U.S., and that was all I knew. I had some friends who went with me to the airport and they told me, "If you see a sign that says, 'Exit,' then you exit there. If you need to go to the bathroom, you will find a bathroom." They said, "If you have any other questions, you can always get help by drawing." That was all the information I had. I hardly understood any English. On the airplane, when people were talking, I could not understand anything, but it happened a family I could talk to was on the plane. They kept saying, "Oh, you are going to get lost" and this just made me nervous.

When I got to Ethiopia, I connected to a plane going to Detroit. It was summer, and I think it was August, and before I left home people told me that in America it is very cold and you could even freeze and die in the house. Because of that, I bought a big jacket that you could wear and cover your face. I spent a lot of money on that jacket that you could wear to keep you warm. When we landed in Detroit, I grabbed my jacket and put it on and put the hood over my head to make sure I was covered because I just knew when I went out I was going to freeze to death. As I was getting out of the plane, I saw in people's eyes that they were shocked because everyone there wore shorts and t-shirts. This guy from Abilene, who had been in Algeria for mission work and was a friend of the ACU track coach, saw me and realized that I was from Africa. He approached me and asked me where I was from. I saw this guy with a big beard, and he sounded funny, and I could not understand what he was saying. He asked me, "Where are you from?" My answer was, "Coach?" He asked, "Where are you going?" I answered, "Coach." Everything he asked me, the answer was "coach" because that was all I knew. Then he asked to see my passport and he looked at it and asked me, "Do you run?" I said, "Yes, I run." Then he went to a phone and put coins in the phone. I had never seen phones that you put coins in and did not know that you could put coins in a phone and make it work. He got on the phone and called the coach at ACU and asked him if he was expecting a runner from Africa. The coach told him "yes," and the man told the coach he would bring me to him. We happened to be on the same flight from Detroit to Dallas and then when we got off the plane in Dallas, he had his truck parked there. I could tell he was confused as to how he was going to tell me he was taking me to Abilene. On the way, I remember that he taught me the word "window." He told me that if I wanted to learn English, I had to learn to spell. I could tell very soon that if I was going to communicate with people, I had to learn how to spell.

On our way to Abilene, he decided to take me to eat at Taco Bueno. This was my first experience at a fast food restaurant, as we did not have these in Rwanda. We went to this restaurant and as I looked at the menu board, there was no single word I ever saw before and nothing that I knew. It was all very strange to me. He told me to pick out a food and I thought about it, but I could not help at all. Finally, I saw something that looked like beans. This looked familiar because beans were an important food at home. However, what I thought was beans was actually ground beef. I ordered tacos – one was soft and one was crispy. I was able to eat the crispy one and then when I started eating the soft taco, everything in it started falling out. I was embarrassed because I did not know how to eat it and the guy was embarrassed. I do not think I ate anything else until we got to Abilene.

As we drove from Dallas to Abilene, I saw the bushes and I thought America did not have any trees. I thought it was just lights and big buildings and streets. I just kept my thoughts to myself, because I did not want to ask the man why there were just bushes beside the road. As we drove, I saw lights from a far distance. This was very unusual because in my country you would not see lights at night, except for maybe in a few places. I could tell that it was dry and I was thirsty and hot, but I saw that the trees were green. This was also very unusual to me. I still had my jacket on because my mind thought that I should be cold.

ABILENE CHRISTIAN UNIVERSITY

I arrived at ACU in August 2005 to pursue my undergraduate degree in psychology. I would run for the ACU track team to pay my way through school. When we got to Abilene, one of the track coaches picked me up and took me to my teammate's apartment. This coach was an old and wise man and he put me in his car. As he drove me toward where we were going, he asked me about my performance. He asked me what my times were in the 5000 meters and the 10,000 meters, and I am sure he was trying to see if I was a good fit for their program.

Martin O'Kello, from Uganda, was my roommate. He spoke a little bit of Swahili and I also spoke a little bit of Swahili, as well. However, I did not understand English. People came to our place and they talked for hours and hours, but I did not understand anything. I believe I got to Abilene on Friday. That night, Martin showed me a place to take a shower and after I showered, as was our culture in Africa, if you have a guest you give them something to eat, so Martin brought in two bottles of soda – one was Sprite and the other was orange. It was rare to have soda at home and I had not had any to drink in a long time, so I thought, "I am hot, I am tired and I am hungry, so I am going to drink this no matter what happens." I remember drinking about three or four glasses of Sprite and after that we relaxed a little bit and then a lot of African people, who lived in Abilene, came to welcome me to America. That night we went to one of my teammate's house to celebrate. There was dancing, eating and fellowship.

In the morning, my roommate, who was also my teammate and who was competing for ACU for a long time, came to me and said, "Serge, let's go for a run." He took me for a 10-mile run and I could tell that he was testing me to see if I was going to be a good runner for ACU because ACU was well-known for its track program. As we ran, he listened to music. He listened to a Walkman. I had never seen this before. I could not believe that this was how people run in America – by listening to music. We finished at the same time and I was still in good shape, so he could tell that I would be a good runner. This was my introduction to ACU.

Later in the day, Derek Hood, the man who was my track coach, came by the apartment to introduce himself and told me that on Monday we would begin practice. I was very excited to start running because this was the reason for my scholarship.

On Monday, Coach Hood came to get me and we went to the opening chapel ceremony for the whole school, which is a traditional program. When we were in chapel, they spoke English and I could not understand anything. I remember they mentioned that we were supposed to stand up, and I did not understand until

Coach nudged me. At that time, they were welcoming the freshman.

Later in the day, I had my first practice with the track team. Practice consisted of a long run – about 10 miles. Coach took us out in the Abilene countryside and we ran and made jokes as we ran. I had teammates who were Kenyan, Burundian and Ugandan, as well as American. Many of us from Africa spoke Swahili, so whenever I wanted to speak to my coach, or make a joke, I asked some of my teammates to translate. It was on this team where my Swahili also improved, as I barely spoke Swahili when I arrived, but now I can speak it well enough that anyone who speaks Swahili can understand. I have been fortunate to be able to learn many languages.

Coach was very nice to me and his coaching and motivation made my running better. I had my first competition in the U.S. in North Carolina, an 8000 meter competition called the "Nike All American." I finished very strong in this race, in a way I never expected. I thought to myself that I would be able to defend my scholarship throughout my undergraduate years. Coach was happy with my performance and I was happy myself.

After I was at ACU a few months, my country sent me an invitation to represent it during the World Championships for a half-marathon in Italy. The Sports Federation at home worked very hard to get me there because they knew I would probably break the country's record. The Secretary and Minister of Sports worked on this. All the people involved in sports in my country were focused on me entering this race. I trained hard so I could go and represent my country – and also have a chance to go and eat some good spaghetti. My country had a ticket ready for me to fly to Italy, but I received a letter from the International Association of Athletics Federation (IAAF) authorizing me to obtain an Italian visa after it was too late to approach the Italian Embassy in the U.S. to get a visa. I was in touch with the embassy and they told me that if I came the next day, they would give me a visa, but that was the day of the competition and so I missed that competition. After that, my focus was training for the Olympic trials. This focus changed my running career because it was during this time that my performance became strong.

I remember when we went to California in November 2005 to run for the NCAA Division II Cross Country Championship, we were going to Hollywood and every-one was very excited. They had cameras to take pic-tures, and I wondered, "What is Hollywood?" When we got there, it was very busy and there were stars of the famous people on the ground. There was a star for Michael Jackson, and a man standing beside it, dressed like him, and I thought, "This is crazy." Next to him was a guy holding a big snake in his arms. I asked, "What is Hollywood?" One of my teammates, who happened to be South-American British, told me that this was where they made all the movies. He told me, "Oh, Serge, this is the place I wanted to see before I die." Later on, we went to Disneyland and the same thing happened. People were taking pictures, jumping over and around and I was thinking, "Oh, my!"

In May 2006, I qualified to run in the NCAA Division II Outdoor Track and Field Championship in the 5000 meters and the 10,000 meters. The meet was held in Emporia, Kan. I was running in the 5000 meters preliminary heat on Friday night, but during the race my feet got hot and slippery inside my shoes. I could tell that my feet were hurting, but I tried to stay with the pack. It got to the point that I could not stand the pain any longer, but even though I wanted to quit, my heart told me to keep running. I kept running in spite of the pain, and was able to finish the race, but I did not do well because of the problems with my shoes and the pain they caused. The shoes caused blisters on my feet, and because of this I did not qualify to run the next day in the 5000 meters final race. Coach asked me to run in the 10,000 meters on Saturday, and I did this in spite of the blisters on my feet. I ran the entire race, but by the time I finished my feet were bleeding and I did not do very well in the race.

We came back to Abilene and I ran in many competitions. The moment that stands out in my mind is the first time that we won a cross country national title. In November 2006, we were in Florida and we had five strong runners on the team. Coach expected us to win the championship. We got to the beach in Pensacola and I wondered in my mind how we would win the championship. We had a swimming pool at the hotel, and Coach came out and told us to please not make ourselves tired. I immediately got out of the water because I wanted to take care of my body.

In the morning we got up and went to race. When we got to the starting line, my teammates said, "Are we all together?" We immediately said, "Yes." We decided to stay together through the whole competition. The gun went off and we started running. A coach was at each corner encouraging us. We kept going and as we got near the end of the race, Coach yelled at me, "Serge, give it your best kick." I started running harder and we crossed the line and won the competition. This was the first time that ACU won a national title in cross country. It was so exciting and as soon as we got back home we started training for the next year's race.

The following spring (2007), at the NCAA Division II Indoor Track and Field Championship in Boston, I was very strong and felt that I would be able to run with anyone at any time. I was entered in the Distance Medley Relay (DMR) and the 5000 meters. I started in the DMR and was my team's first leg. I was to run 1200 meters and pass the baton to the 800-meter guy. I was in second place when I passed the baton. My coach was proud of me because it was my first time to run the DMR, and running 1200 meters as a long-distance person was not usual. I was also happy with myself because I contributed that much to the team. We were in the position to win the DMR but one of our teammates was bumped and fell down, and we ended up fourth as a team. The next day, I was to run the 5000 meters, and I was very excited. I wanted to win that race so badly because I was very strong, and I was in a good mood and thought I would win. After a mile and a half, my shoes, which have never been a good friend of my legs, started to bother me. I was in front of the pack and I could feel a big blister on my foot. I said to myself, "I will never quit." I ran and ran and with about 1000 meters to go, I felt blood and heat inside my shoes. I still did not want to quit. Coach was on the corner and I told him that I had a blister and it was so bad. I think Coach told me to stop, but I was in a good position to finish in the top 10, so I kept running and finished with points for our team. When I finished the race, Coach came to me and I took off my shoes and he saw that the skin of my feet was rubbed off. He was shocked and thought I fought hard. The trainer treated my feet, but after I got home, they still had not healed. When a friend of mine saw them, he took me to the hospital. My feet were infected and so I needed antibiotics to treat them. Before long, though, I was back to running.

The season after this I was even stronger and I qualified for the 2007 NCAA Division II Outdoor Track and Field Championship in the 5000 meters and 10,000 meters. However, a month before time for the national championships, the NCAA handed down penalties to the ACU track program for some violations. I was not allowed to attend the championship meet because of the ride I received from the Dallas airport and the ride my friend gave me to the hospital. I was not aware that I violated any NCAA rules, but this did not stop them from penalizing me. ACU went on to win the outdoor national championship that year.

After these penalties, I went out for the fall cross country team. When we started running for cross country in fall 2007, I felt very healthy and very strong. We had some hard workouts, as usual. In the middle of the season, the number one guy on our team got a knee injury and Coach told me I had to step up and be the number one guy. I had great confidence, even though my other teammates were very strong. I worked hard and went on to win the conference championship and the regional championship, and as a result received the Male Athlete of the Year for the NCAA Division II South Central Region award. By winning these championships, it assured our team a place at the cross country national championship, which seemed like a dream after our best runner was injured.

The 2007 regional championship was held in Joplin, Mo., and I will never forget how I flew during the regional meet. I was in good shape and had no pain and no fear. I could tell that coach saw potential in me, and when we went back to Missouri for nationals in November 2007, Coach approached me and said, "Serge, if anybody starts slowing down, go ahead and go and win the championship." As I was defending my championship from conference and region, I thought I would win the national championship as well. We started running and I was in front of the pack, breathing well, moving my arms and legs as much as I wanted, and leading the pack most of the time. After the 8000 meter mark, I was still with the group, leading some, passing through the bush, and climbing hills. As we went to finish, I saw the finish line, and everyone started kicking. Two guys took off and I took off as number three, but as I came around the corner getting ready to run straight to the finish, two guys passed by. I tried to get ahead of them again, but it was too late, and I ended up being number six. But I was not disappointed at all because we wanted to win the national championship and my points contributed to the national title. We ended up winning the national title again, for the second year in a row. We celebrated the second national title of my collegiate career in my third year at ACU. From that time on, I received e-mails from the Rwandan Minister of Sports encouraging me to participate for my country.

In spring 2008, I qualified for the NCAA Division II Outdoor Track and Field Championship in the 5000 meters and 10,000 meters. The meet was held at Saint Augustine's University in North Carolina. I finished at number seven in the finals of the 5000 meters.

In fall 2008, I again ran cross country. What our team experienced that season will never be erased from my memory. Our team was composed of five strong African runners, who trained hard to win nationals three years in a row. We won conference, as was our tradition, and won region, as was our tradition as well. Everyone was ready to win that national title again. Unfortunately, the national meet was held in Pittsburg, Penn., where the temperature was 19 degrees Fahrenheit. You can imagine African guys, who have never been in any weather that is below 50 degrees in their whole lives, and taking them to weather that is 19 degrees, where they have to warm up and then run 10,000 meters. We got to Pennsylvania on Friday evening, and the weather was cold, but not too bad. We expected the weather to be cold in the morning. In the morning, we woke up, ate breakfast and headed to the course. As soon as we got to the course, we were afraid to get out of the van. Everyone had on about three coats. Coach said, "Get out!" As we got out, we started freezing, and as we were looking around, here were white kids, naked. That is when we sensed that something bad was going to happen. We wondered why everyone was naked on top; just a few Africans were the only ones who were frozen. We started doing warm-ups, but never got warm even with our three jackets on. I remember my teammates and me running back into this small house that was provided for officials to stay warm during the competition. We were trying to get warm – to warm out feet, our hands – but the house was too small for all the

Africans from different teams, and the Americans who were also cold. At that time, we were about to start the race, and everyone was scared of taking off their clothes. I remember taking off my jacket that I wore when I came to the U.S., and putting a lot of Vaseline on my body, thinking that it would save me. We started running, and as we were running, at every corner I struggled to keep running. Most of the guys from Africa I knew, who were very strong, were just standing instead of running, and every time I got to the corner Coach told me to keep running. I remember I smiled a little bit while I ran, and then I could not close my mouth, so I finished the whole race with my mouth open because I could not close it again. Every time I got in front of Coach, he said, "Serge, you look good!" Maybe it was because I was smiling. Finally, we came to the finish line and every African person I knew was down. Some were crying, some were unconscious – and I could never explain this to anyone. It made me feel like Pittsburg is not a place.

"The Voice of America," the radio station that broadcasts in Kinyarwanda, knew I was running and they called me the next morning to find out about the race. They interviewed me before I went and I told them that Pittsburg was very cold and we were not able to move our legs, so this was not good news for me, my team and my country. We went back home and I am sure that Coach did not blame us because it was a natural weakness we could not avoid.

In spring 2009, I was running well, but at the conference championships, I received an injury while running in the 10,000 meters and as a result my collegiate running career came to an end.

During my track career at ACU, I achieved the following awards:

- U.S. Track & Field and Cross Country Coaches Association All-American - 2006, 2007
- All-Lone Star Conference Team - 2006, 2007, 2008 and 2009
- Lone Star Conference Champion – 2007
- NCAA Division II South Central Region Cross Country Champion - 2007
- NCAA Division II South Central Region Cross Country Male Athlete of the Year - 2007
- Trinidad/Tobago Venture 5K participant - September 2008

My first class at ACU was an English class, which I took as an English-as-a-Second-Language (ESL) student, and that class began my academic journey in the U.S. I remember our teacher told us how to teach ourselves English after classes by listening to cartoons and watching Disney movies (they had simple and soft English). I kept that idea until now and as soon as I got home, I asked my roommate how to get kids' movies. He showed me the Box Office store where I could go to rent movies. I watched movies and read the news over and over again. Every day I could see my English getting better and better. We had a lot of writing compositions and I could see how this was changing my life and improving my English skills. My teacher was proud and after one semester I could read and speak and write English. She decided that I should go ahead and take regular classes after that. I remember that I started with an Old Testament Bible class. In that class, I could tell that the things I understood were maybe one out of a hundred and the only way I could pass the class was to memorize the whole thing – I memorized verses and I memorized long and complicated names from the Bible. Every time I would see a word that I had memorized, I would think about everything I had learned about that word. I ended up finishing the semester and doing well in that class because of the motivation I had and the encouragement I received from my professor. I was working on doing well in my classes and I have never had less than a 3.0 grade point average (GPA).

I struggled at times, because it was hard to wake up at 5 a.m. and go run out of Abilene and then come back to Abilene around 7:30 a.m., take a shower and have to be in class by 8 a.m. After class, I was working at an on-campus job and then at 3 p.m. I would go to track practice until 6 p.m. Then I would go back to work for two more hours and then I had a lot of home-work waiting for me. I would have to find people to help me with my home-work, and a lot of time these people would tell me they were busy and would not be free until 2 a.m. I had no choice but to wait until they were available, so for my first two years I hardly got any sleep. The school had tutors available, but I had to have someone who could speak French or Kinyarwanda, and if I could not find a tutor, I would spend the night on the computer using a Website that would translate French to English. Because of this, I remember writing an essay and when I submitted it to my professor, who also happened to speak German, she recognized that it was more of a French style than English. That's when I decided that I needed to find friends who could help me and to learn from them when they were speaking.

I remember asking one of my friends to find me an American student who would be willing to read my compositions and revise them. These were not school assignments, but writings I would do to improve my English skills.

All of this time, I had track competitions going on outside of Abilene, and this meant that we would leave on Friday evening and come back on Sunday morning or evening. I was blessed by this, because it meant that I was able to travel across much of the U.S. and I got to see many states.

I knew that God had a plan for me for me to survive the genocide, but I did not know that I would ever speak English. When I got to ACU in 2005 it was my first time trying to explain myself in English. Yes, indeed it was hard but I sat down and worked hard and now I can write a research paper of many pages with no problem.

Being exposed to the ACU classes and the Abilene community changed my life tremendously. Just the fact that people were nice and helpful and were Christians, I thought about that a lot. I thought about the fact that my sense of humor was gone and I felt that I needed to change a lot in my life. I felt that I wanted to change and to make a difference in other people's lives, if I could. I can never adequately express what ACU and the Abilene community have done for me. They helped me at a time when I knew there was no relationship between me and them. It made me think of those children in Rwanda who were suffering but who had no one to care about them.

I decided that I would always have these children in my mind, and I wanted to do something to help them.

My eligibility to run for ACU was almost over and in December 2008, I went back to Rwanda for about a month. I was there with one of my American friends who was visiting Rwanda at that time. I went home and worked with some children who were my age who had lost their parents and were responsible for their own homes, and sometimes taking care of younger siblings. There was a group called Extra Mile that was helping them survive. There was also an American missionary there who was working with Extra Mile. While in Kigali, I met the founder of this group. I had a meeting with the leaders to learn more about what they were doing, and we had a trip to visit Nyamata and see some children there. We were looking for ways to find jobs for the orphans who might be living in Kigali, so they could attend university there. We worked on a few projects at that time, we met for prayers and tried to develop a strategy plan for the future. We also helped develop a test for them in English, so they would be able to communicate with foreigners who might give them jobs. It was an amazing trip and an exciting opportunity.

I came back to the United States and finished my running career with ACU and graduated from ACU in the spring of 2009 with a Bachelor of Science in Psychology. By the time I graduated, I knew I wanted to go back home to work with children, but I also knew that I could have more influence if I had more education for them to relate to.

During my undergraduate tenure, I received some special awards from ACU. In 2007, I received the Fighting

Heart Award, which is presented to a student-athlete who advanced themselves both on and off the field without recognition or accolades. In 2007, I also received a Christian Servant Award, which is given in honor of upholding the principles, philosophy and example of servant-leadership. I was also named to Who's Who Among Students in American Universities & Colleges in 2007 and 2008, an award given in recognition of outstanding merit and accomplishment as a student. In 2009, I was awarded the Dean Adams Achievement Award, which is awarded for recognition of exemplary character, outstanding academic achievement and determined perseverance to overcome obstacles to obtain education.

ABILENE FRIENDSHIPS

I made many friends while at ACU and some of them stand out in particular ways. I remember that when I was sitting in the stadium at the outdoor championships in Emporia in May 2006, a pretty girl was sitting beside me and she started talking to me. She introduced herself to me and told me she was an ACU student also. Her name was Tori Watson, and I could tell that she was a person who was very interested in sports. She was a very nice girl, and her parents were sitting in front of us. She introduced me to her parents, the Watsons, and I remember that we had a long conversation that night. This family was very nice and from that time our relationship deepened. On the final day, I remember we were sitting in the same place and I remember her mom asked me a lot of questions about where I was from and I asked her questions, as well. After that we became friends, and Tori invited me to Abilene events. I remember that she invited me to go to the 4th of July celebration with her. I had never seen fireworks before.

One thing I will never forget about Tori is when it was hot in the summer and she said, "We need to go get a snow cone." I thought she was saying ice cream because I had never had a snow cone, so I asked her what she was talking about. I asked her to repeat that again, and I still could not understand what she was talking about. After a while, she realized that there was no way I was going to understand what she was talking about so she started trying to explain to me by using gestures or signs. I remember that she started by saying, "They get ice and shave the ice and it becomes small; then they put corn syrup over it." I asked her, "What is corn syrup?" and she tried explaining that it is a liquid that comes from various fruits and it has the flavor of those fruits, and then they spray it on top of the ice. We went to get a snow cone and when I tasted it, it was, of course, cold. I never liked cold things, but I tasted it and it was sweet, so I enjoyed it because it was sweet. The more I sipped on it, the more I liked it. Because Tori is the one who introduced me to the snow cone, I never went by myself to buy one. Now it has become the symbol of our friendship, whenever she is in town we go together to get a snow cone.

Since then, I have been the whole family's friend. They have a heart for people and they have a heart for the kids in Africa, as they have been supportive of my efforts to raise money to provide health care for children in Africa. Something I remember about this family is that on many occasions like Christmas, Thanksgiving, Halloween and Easter (many of the holidays on the American calendar), I went to their home for dinner. A couple of times they took me with them to get a Christmas tree at a Christmas tree farm, which was many miles away. They also took me to the Pumpkin Patch, which was a place you could go buy pumpkins and was hosted by Disability Resources, a program for mentally challenged adults. Up to now, I am still good friends with this family, and we are in the same church group. One thing I learned from this family is that their hospitality is amazing. Since I started going to their house, I was not always there by myself. There were other people there and everyone was allowed to share their thoughts and express themselves. They listen and everyone is welcomed. I feel this is a characteristic many people should have. This is a place, also, that I get my wounds healed because it is good to see people who are not judgmental or who do not take you back to bad memories. It is a good place that I could go and feel good if something was wrong during that day. I hope to put my foot in their steps one day.

In May 2006, at the end of my freshman year, I met a student named Ryan Campbell. I met Ryan on campus at ACU. He was good friends with two guys from Ghana, and there was a banquet for graduate students and these students invited me to the banquet. Ryan was also a graduate student. I noticed that he made a lot of jokes and could tell he was a fun person to be around. He approached me and introduced himself to me, and I could tell that he was interested in knowing me.

The guys' plans for after graduation were going to Oplin, to what is called the "Grand Ole Oplin." This is a place where the community gathers to dance to country music. There are people of all ages – young children, old people and everyone in between. There were people ninety years old and I thought it was interesting to see someone that old dancing to country music. It was a very nice environment because there was no smoking and no drinking. People just drank sodas and ate chips. Oplin is a popular place for people from Abilene to go. Ryan was there dancing the Two-Step. I was single at the time, and two girls there taught me to dance the Two-Step. I had a cowboy hat, but had on dress pants, while everyone else was in cowboy jeans, so you could tell that I was not from that culture. Those two girls did a very good job of teaching me to dance the Two-Step and the Chicken Dance. I remember we ended the dancing that night with the Chicken Dance. Everyone does that dance together, and you hold on to each other. At the end of the dance, I did not want to go home. I felt loved, and the environment felt perfect to me, so I did not want to leave. We went home after that, and Ryan was laughing at my dancing and impressed with how I was able to immerse myself in that culture and have fun.

Ryan was interested in meeting me another time for coffee. We became friends and he called me and came to see me, and our friendship kept growing. We picked a day to meet, and he asked me where I lived. I told him, and he told me his roommate was leaving and asked me to be his roommate. I had always wanted an American roommate, so I could learn how to live with someone from a different background. Because I saw him to be a very open and outgoing person, I decided to go and live with him.

In August, I moved in with Ryan. Living with Ryan taught me a lot of things. Ryan is a person who knows how to live with others without considering where they come from, their color, their accent, their beliefs and their values. He is very open, optimistic and an achiever. I remember seeing him study all night when he was supposed to be in class at 8 a.m., and he was up until 3 a.m. I woke up and saw Ryan still studying, and I learned from him that I must work hard and I learned a good work ethic from him. Ryan always had everything written down on a schedule. This is when I decided that I would always learn from everyone – poor people, rich people, smart people, people who do not consider themselves smart. Ryan always said that all people are created in the image of God and Ryan believes that. I think this is a lesson I learned from Ryan. He did not get angry a lot, and I believe I became a better person by observing how Ryan controlled his anger and because he was such an easy-going person.

I grew up as a Catholic, but because of how Catholic members acted during the genocide I ended up losing my faith. Because of his personality, it was easy for Ryan to help me transform from a non-Christian person to a Christian person. We do not always have to teach people with words – teaching them with our actions is some-times much better because this is how Ryan brought me to God. I met his parents a couple of times and he took me to church with him. I was going to church and seeing people be nice to me, but I never forgot what had happened to me at the church in Ntarama. At this time, I still thought that humans were created evil. Whenever someone was nice to me, I thought that it was probably a trick and tomorrow they would try to hurt me. The fact that people who were our neighbors and friends came to slaughter us was still in my mind. I was in Abilene almost a year without going to church. I watched Ryan going to church many times when I stayed home, but after watching him go to church I decided to start going with him. One day Ryan got in the car and said, "Let's go to church," so I got in the car with him and we went to church. One day when we were driving to church, Ryan asked me if I ever thought of being baptized. He asked me this after a long time of prayers and spiritual conversations. I thought in my heart, "This is the time, tomorrow is not yours." As soon as we got to the church, I was baptized and immediately I felt that my soul was more clean. Since then, I cannot tell you how much my life has changed.

In December 2006, Ryan was going to his parents for Christmas and he said, "Serge, do you have anybody here to go with for Christmas while I am gone?" I told him, "No," and he called a leader from the church he was attending and asked him if he would pick me up so I could be with them at Christmas. Mr. Vann and Mrs. Susan Conwell came to pick me up on Christmas Day and I went with them to the home of one of their friends, where we had dinner. I think this was the best Christmas I ever had because everyone was so nice and we played games. One of the games used a lot of English words, and at that time my English vocabulary was very short and I was not fluent in English, so it was a way for me to learn new words. I remember that one of the words used in the game was "apple."

Because of this time spent together, I connected with this family, and they became like adoptive parents to me. They helped develop my character because of the way the family is a family of God. They have a heart for people and it is not just me, I think it is everyone. Seeing the way they treat people the same is also in my memory. They advise me when I am thinking wrong and I also ask them for advice when I have decisions to make. They are my parents, and at the same time, they are my mentors and my inspiration.

This family became more and more important to me as I was growing spiritually, emotionally and psychologically. They are the people I can look to when something goes wrong. I always observe them because I feel like anything I can learn from them can be useful in my life. The whole family works hard, including my sisters. They have a heart for people and God and display this in the way they always help people who are in need. When I saw that my adopted dad is a leader in church, who many people trust and like his work, it made me feel that I should be a servant of God the rest of my life. They are humble and generous. I feel comfortable when I am sitting with them, asking them advice and I go to them for counseling. They are not judgmental and are always by my wife's and my side, no matter if we are right or wrong. One thing I will never forget about this family is that sometimes my adopted mom surprised me with text messages in the middle of the week, saying, "How are you doing son and daughter?" They always close their text messages with, "We love you, son and daughter." They healed a lot of wounds in my life and I only hope that one day I will be such an example that other people can look up to.

Another person who made a big impact in my life was Shane McClung, the man who drove me to Abilene from the Dallas airport when I first came to the U.S. Shane has been on many mission trips to Africa, but has not been to Rwanda. Shane is generous and works very, very hard. Just being near him, I was amazed by how hard he works. He is a man of strong principles and his principles make him unique. Shane thinks independently and does not depend on what others around him may be doing or thinking. We became very good friends, although many times we looked at things very differently and often had to compromise our way of looking at things to come to agreement. This is one thing I appreciate about my friendship with him. Two things Shane taught me are to never quit and never have an excuse. These were very good lessons to me because I try not to quit on myself and not to make excuses. This is a principle that has been very important to me since the genocide.

During my sophomore year at ACU, a guy from Houston heard about me from a friend of mine who lives in Dallas and called me and said, "Serge, there is a new family from Africa that came to Abilene, and I heard that you are from Africa and you live in Abilene." He asked me to go visit the new family, and this request forever changed my life. I told the guy I would go see the family and went to visit them. When I visited them, only the father and some small children were there. The rest of the family was at a place where they could learn English. When I visited with the father, I learned that he was from Congo and had lost a lot of people from his family through wars in his country, so they came to the U.S. as refugees. When it was almost time to go home, I saw a group of people coming in. Among them was a beautiful, quiet girl. She caught my eye immediately. I introduced myself to the whole family and visited with them a little bit before leaving. As is customary in my culture, the whole family went outside to walk with me to send me home. I went back to campus. Since I was a sophomore in college at this time, I thought I still had too far to go in school to start dating. I continued to be involved with my running and my academic career. During this time, I developed a relationship with the girl's uncle, but I did not know at that time that he was related to her.

When I was a senior and almost ready to graduate, I thought to myself, "I need to go back and see if that girl is still around." Since her uncle became my friend, he went with me to visit her family. When I got to her home, she was sick. When it was time for us to leave, I said, "Let me say a prayer," and I prayed for her. The next day, I called her to ask how she was doing. The conversation started from there. She called me and I called her. I was still very busy with school and with running, but I made time to see her. After about six months of talking to each other, we started dating. After we started dating, I was very serious about my feelings for her, and she seemed to be very serious, too, about me. Then, I initiated the thought of being together for the rest of our lives. This is how it is back home – you do not surprise a girl with a ring. You start a conversation and see if they take it or refuse it. I started talking to her and wanted to see how she thought. She was someone who was very serious. Sometimes I would test her to see how she would react to things. I tried to put obstacles in front of her, testing her temper and other things. However, I did not make her cry. After many, many tests, we talked and our goals were almost the same. She is a woman of God and she is trustworthy. She loves people, which is most important to me and she is very smart. So, after we talked about living together for the rest of our lives, as is the custom in our culture, she went to talk to her parents. When her parents heard about our relationship, they received the news well.

I remember that this was a few months before I decided that I wanted to go home and see children who were suffering and experiencing the life that I had lived, who did not have a job and did not have what I had. My mission for that trip was to see if I could do something for the children there using what I learned at ACU and to work for housing for children from the genocide, but I also used the trip to meet my girlfriend's family. Since I was planning a trip to Rwanda, her parents told me that I should talk to her older sister over there and introduce myself and see what others in the family thought, as is customary in our culture. They approved of our relationship, also. When I came back to the U.S., we started a very, very serious conversation of how we planned to live together in one year. Her family, as it is always done, decided upon the bride prize, which was to be twelve cows, as was customary in our culture. Cows are a symbol of a strong promise and a good relationship. Her family in Rwanda talked to her family in the U.S. and behind the scenes agreed that I was able to marry her. As soon as I got back to the U.S., I approached her father to find out if it was true that I would get the girl. He said that I would get the girl, and the next day I told my family and relatives back in Rwanda that I would be getting a wife and to get ready to deliver the bride prize. My family in Rwanda got twelve cows and delivered them to my future bride's sister in Rwanda. After that, we got more and more serious and we set a wedding date, and dowry date and the dream became a reality on July 24, 2010.

Serge Gasore and Victoria Watson with Lorin Watson in background at Christmas Tree Farm in America.

Serge and Esperance Gasore on their wedding day with Serge's adopted family, Vann & Susan Conwell, Caroline and Katie Lea Conwell.

PIVOTAL MOMENTS – MY DAY TO DIE

Many things happened to me that you might call "pivotal events" in my life. Each of these affected me deeply and in different ways. There was the death of my mother, witnessing the death of my grandmother, surviving the church bombing and weeks of running and hiding in the jungle, just foraging for food and struggling to stay alive. There was witnessing the death of family members. There were the deaths of so many of my family – some I was very close to and some not as close. There was life in the RPF. There was the end of the normal, peaceful and happy life I enjoyed prior to the genocide, and the struggle returning to a normal life after the genocide.

Another event that I see as a significant part of my life occurred when I was captured and taken into Congo. One day I happened to go visit my uncle Eugene, who lived near the school I attended. On my way there, I was walking and a white Toyota Corolla came past me and pulled over. Three guys were inside, and they stopped and lowered the window and asked me if I knew a certain person they were looking for. After I told them that I knew where this person lived, they asked me if I minded taking them there. It was a Saturday morning, and I got into the car, and as soon as I got into the car, they immediately rolled up the windows and two guys turned to me and grabbed my arms and pulled them behind my back. At this time I did not take it as a joke because death was still very real to me, and that idea I had about human beings being created evil was settled in my mind and was still alive. After being thrown in the car, in my mind I said, "This is the time for me to die," but I cannot remember if I was scared because my heart became senseless right after the genocide and I did not get it back until a few years ago. However, despite the fact that I denied Him after seeing people hacked to death inside the church, I asked God that I be taken to heaven if died. My kidnappers had a needle with medicine in it, and they stuck it in my arm and I immediately lost consciousness. I could not think enough to know that there was no way I could fight back. Because this happened near where I had a lot of relatives, they made me write a letter that said, "This is revenge for what you have done to us." They threw the letter through the window at a bus stop near where my relatives lived. Someone took the letter to my relatives and the news was all over the place that I was captured. I remember that we drove through Kigali. I could see people, but I had no way to talk to them and no energy to fight back. We went to the border of Rwanda and Congo, and entered Congo. When we got into Congo, they parked somewhere and we travelled into the bush. This was a huge, huge bush. When we got into the bush, there were a lot of guys drinking and partying and having a lot of fun moments. When I got there, it was like when Jesus was taken to

Pilate for persecution. They made fun of me, they took all of my clothes and I was naked, and they tied my hands behind my back and made me lie down facing the sun. I lived with them for three days. They gave me food. The thing I most appreciated about them during this time was that they fed me, which brought me hope, because my mind told me that I would survive like I survived the genocide attacks. I still regret that during that time it was hard for me to recognize that God was the one doing all of this. I was there for three days, and snakes were my friends. They crawled by me, but none of them bit me. On the first day, snakes crawled by and I thought, "Oh, he is going to get me, he is going to get me." On the second day, I said the same thing. After that, I wasn't afraid anymore. Every day, though, I thought it was my day to die.

I was close to becoming blind from facing the sun and I had no way to roll over. During the day, they made sure that my eyes were open. During those three days of captivity, each day felt like a hundred days. When the sun came up, I was excited that it was daytime, but at the same time I was worried that it was time to face the sun. I tried to turn over to avoid the sun, but they pushed me back over, so that I had to face the sun.

Rolling me over when my arms were tied together reminded me of my Tutsi neighbors and the newlywed couples who were tied together before they were thrown in the river or burned to death. When I was sleeping on my back facing the sun, it seemed like I was reviewing the genocide because visions of all the dead bodies I saw during the genocide continued to occur and it seemed like I was watching a television, and everything smelled like blood. I must also admit that those images of dead people still haunt me, especially during the month of April when the entire world commemorates the genocide. During my captivity, a picture of my kindergarten teacher lying down dead haunted me, and I envisioned myself being in the same situation.

I only got one meal a day, and this was at 4 p.m. After that, the jungle started to smell very funny because of the wind. It started to get dark, dogs began barking and the snakes went away. The guys came back from where they had been for the whole day. They made jokes for a while before they disappeared again for the night. They switched shifts, so that one guy would stay, and the others left with just one guy left to guard me. The routine for those three days was exactly the same each day. In my mind I thought, "Why don't I just tell them to kill me?" On the second day, I thought this, and a voice came to my mind that said, "Serge, don't quit. It is not your time yet. Don't ever give up on your life." I thought that if they fed me, they were about to let me go. I was about to tell them to go ahead and kill me, and the voice came to me again. On the third day, it was my day to die. They all came to me and said "good-bye," mocking me. One of them was given the responsibility to take my life. He was given a gun, and he took me nearby to kill me. We took off with me knowing that I would be killed, and for sure I was not fearful. Instead, I was naive enough to wonder how it felt to be shot, and I wondered whether my extended family would ever see me again. I even wondered if I would be buried or if my dead body would be left out for wild animals to eat. I wished that my relatives would know how I died, despite how obvious it was. However, on our way to the death scene, my guard was talking to me, and he said,

"Serge, these people have killed many people and I don't know if I should stay with them." When we got to where he was supposed to kill me, he said, "Serge, I am going to let you go and I will also have to find my way out of this place, or they will kill me, too." This huge guy said, "See you later. Serge, I hope that one day we will meet again." After I was left there in the middle of the bush, I started thinking how I was going to get out of this jungle. In the bush, I heard the big voice of a truck. The truck was driving from Congo to Rwanda. That was when I decided I would follow the voice of the truck and hope I could reach the road before he passed by. I struggled to get there and I could hear that the trail was so far. I was naked and I had wounds everywhere because I fell on stones as I made my way through the bush. I was in pain, and bleeding everywhere but I kept thinking that this was another opportunity for me to live for a few more hours. This was a jungle and it was very rare for a car to pass there, but I managed to get by the street before the truck passed by. Once I got there, I immediately fell in the street. I thought, "I am going to wait in the street because if he stops it will be by the grace of God." I raised my arms and I heard the sound of the trailer and I could tell it was going so fast, I thought it was going to hit me. Then the driver saw me and he immediately tried to stop the trailer. When he stopped, he got out and was speaking Swahili, and I did not understand Swahili, but I could speak French and he could speak French. He kept speaking to me in Swahili, and I kept speaking to him in French. He went back to his truck, and got a scarf to dress me because I was still naked at this time. He got me some shoes and got me inside the trailer. I was very hungry, thirsty, tired and exhausted. I could not talk very well and my eyes were almost blind. He realized that the only place he could take me was to the border because there was a chance people from my country would be there. When we got to the border, the people learned who I was and where I came from. Before they took me to my home town, however, they took me to the hospital because I needed fluids to restore my body to normal and they gave me food. After this, they took me back to my home.

When I got to my place, everyone was mourning for me and they were holding a wake for me. At this time, people who loved me were suffering, thinking that I was dead already. This same thing had happened to many people besides me. Those other people never came back, and this is why there was no hope that I would come back.

When I got there, nobody asked me what happened to me – they were just celebrating that I was alive. After a while, it became a celebration for the whole area.

THE AFTERMATH

Three things stay in my mind – the dead bodies that I have seen, the images and the smell of the genocide, and the smell of the cows.

I consider the smell of the cows as a good thing because it brings to mind good times for me, as I was around them for so long. The smell of cows reminds me of my grandmother and the house boy who took a special interest in me. It reminds me of those moments in the evenings when we went to meet the cows in their pen to milk them and take their calves to nurse. It reminds me of walking from school and smelling the cows of my neighbor, who was always there. It reminds me of the cows mooing in the evenings when it was dark and quiet. It reminds me that milk was my favorite drink and that my grandmother always made sure I had milk to drink after my meals. It reminds me when people were giving cows to each other as gifts of honor, and we sang songs called *Ibyivugo* for the cows.

One of those songs goes like this: Ruvubu yivugiye kumuvumba bukeye ruvuzo ibyara umuvanda gicuba kinka ntugacubangane gicaniro kinka ntugasinzire. This song says you are praising the cows by reminding the cows how wonderful they are because they produce milk and they should be taken care of all the time.

When I think of the genocide, I see bodies in the river. I see them floating down the river and more bodies, coming and going. I see couples that were killed. I remember one —the couple that was going to get married, and they killed them in their wedding clothes and ran a stick through them and threw them in the water. I remember the woman who was killed and her newborn twins were around her body, crying and trying to get breast milk for several days. I remember seeing one of those children dying and one staying alive, crawling around the mother's dead body. I remember sleeping in the bamboo beside the river and being beside the body that was in the water, and knowing that it was my favorite teacher. I remember the woman coming to me and telling me to get money off her husband's body. I remember my grandmother being blown away by a grenade. I remember going back to the church and seeing the bodies of my relatives and my neighbors just stacked in piles. I remember walking inside the church and walking on top of dead bodies, some lying on their backs, some lying on their stomachs, bleeding from their nose or their mouth. I remember coming from the hiding place and seeing bodies alongside of the street – some still breathing and some calling our names if they heard our voice. That was so sad. I remember one time it was raining and I was running and people were being shot beside me and they just fell down. Some died immediately and others bled to death. I remember coming from my hiding place, going through dead bodies trying to find my relatives and they were nowhere to be found. I remember watching my uncle die from many cuts. I remember dogs hunting us, and when we visited Gatete's hole, the dogs chased us, and we shot them to protect ourselves.

My experience of living through the genocide also changed the way I react when my body receives an injury. I do not look at injuries the way many people who have not lived through a war do. Because I was injured so seriously during the genocide, I did not see injuries I received later as being serious. I saw a lot of wounds and so I do not think of seeking medical treatment when something simple happens to me.

For example, my uncle's wife had an injury that started on the bottom of her feet. It got worse and kept going up on her leg, but she was not able to receive any treatment for it. It eventually got better and healed itself. Another example is the lady that I hid in the mud, and I stepped on her as hard as I could. She is still alive and is normal.

Still another example is what happened to my cousin Eric. They cut his leg with a machete, and I saw maggots inside his wounds but his leg healed. I had wounds on my leg and my head, and they almost healed themselves before I could get treatment. I slept in my own blood and yet came out fine, so that is why it is hard for me to think that when I have a small cut or scratch that it could become infected.

During the time I was a student at ACU, I remember one day at work I spilled hot grease and burned my leg. I did not think too much about this, but I called my friend and asked her if she had some aloe vera plant I could put on the burn. When my friend saw the burn, she was upset and said that I needed to see a doctor because the burn was very bad and could become infected. I did not think about this because the injuries and wounds I saw during the genocide were so much worse than this.

The things that happened during the genocide have also impacted how I live with people because I do not understand how people get mad so easily. I can hardly be mad with the people who killed my grandmother in front of me. If I cannot get mad at the people who killed my grandmother, how can I get mad at someone who cuts in front of me in line at Wal-Mart? How can I be mad at my teacher who gave me a bad grade, when I know there is not a machete or hammer in front of my head? It is hard to understand how some people can get so mad when something so small happens.

I like the expression that says, "Prepare for the worst and hope for the best." I think that things will not always be the way we want them. In life, things change, so we should be prepared for these changes. Streets have corners, and streets can be slippery when it rains. Life takes unexpected twists and turns sometimes. Just sitting back and finding a resolution to your problem and thinking how you can make things in the world better is better than getting angry.

I am also still more cautious in relationships because of the way my neighbors turned on me, and the way husbands turned on their wives. People that we shared food with, and fellowshipped with and had fun with, turned against us and killed us, and this made me feel that man was created evil. Now, because of the good people I mentioned in my story who changed me in a good way, I can feel that humans are created good and they have restored my faith and trust. Now I am working to be more open and to build my character and become a person that God and people around me can appreciate.

There are always obstacles when you try reconciling with people who did bad things to you, but it has been a very good experience because now I can get along with people who consider themselves to be different from me, even if they hurt me in the past. It always makes me happy when we can talk again and forget what separated us in the past and try to become one again because this is what God wants from us as humans.

During the time I was writing the book, I learned that my boss (from the RPF) passed away. While I was writing the book, I talked with him. The first time that I called him, he said, "Oh, my son, you finally called me! You know you should call me as many times as possible." I said, "Yes, I got here to America and I got busy with school." We were talking about the past and remembering the time we were together, I asked him about Kabalisa (a guy I lived with while I was in the RPF) and he told me that Kabalisa passed away in a traffic accident. I did not know that he became a truck driver after he left the service. That was very sad news for me because this was a person I lived with in a very tough time. I remember when I was living with Frank, I lived with Kabalisa at the same time. There were three of us living together, and Kabalisa and I were both Frank's escorts.

I have great memories of Kabalisa. For example, one day we were working in an abandoned house and land mines were on the ground. I saw a land mine and was about to step on it, so I asked him why he did not warn me about the land mine. He said he did not tell me because he wanted me to step on it and loose one leg, and then I would be more careful about the other leg. I knew that he did not mean that, but he was always joking and his jokes had something to be learned. I knew he was always trying to make sure that I was careful. I remember he told me one time that even if he saw me trying to touch a fire he would not warn me because he wanted me to be careful. Hearing that he passed away was a shock to me. Kabalisa was about ten to fifteen years older than I, and I thought of him as being very old because I was so young when I lived with him.

It was not until after a year after my boss' death that I received an e-mail from my cousin Bosco saying that my "Afande" (which means "boss") died. I was still in school and we just had a baby, and it took a while to find out why he died. I called Rwanda and tried to find out about him, but when I called somebody picked up the phone but they did not answer. I found out that he died from complications of diabetes. Since I received this news, my heart goes back to the past a lot and I remember the tough times when we lived together, and none of them were happy when I was feeling bad and vice versa. In fact, there was a time my salary was not coming through and Kabalisa brought my salary when I really, really needed it. My salary was 6,000 FRW (Rwandan money) which equals about $10 (U.S.) per month. My honest feelings are that now that the people I lived with have died, I am next and I think this a lot. I feel that those people who lived at that time are leaving and I often wonder if I am next.

I wanted to go to my boss and tell him face-to-face, "Thank you," and maybe give him some cows to honor him and show him my appreciation. When I mentioned this to my adopted mom, Susan, she told me that what I could do is "pay it forward." I know that Frank has children who are still living, and I would like to reach out to them and let them know how grateful I am to him. I was able to speak with Frank only one time after I came to the U.S., but I kept up with him through my uncle who also lived in Kigali where Frank lived.

I do not fear death because I know that God knows there are things I am here to accomplish, and I know that when I die it will mean that I have accomplished what God has planned for me. It just gives me a feeling of sadness and emptiness to know that these men who meant so much to me at such a difficult time in my life are no longer on this earth. It seems to me that as I get older the things that happened during the genocide are coming back to me more. It seems that everyone who was kind to me in my life has died – my mother, my grandmother, my boss, Kabalisa, and other relatives – and sometimes I am prone to wonder if the same thing will be happening now. I wonder if those who are close to me will be taken from me in a short time. I do not think this is true because there are many people who care about me, but sometimes I am inclined to wonder about this.

EPILOGUE - LOOKING TO THE PAST FOR THE FUTURE

My transition after the genocide was hard. After the genocide, I felt I lost myself. I lost my faith. I lost much of my family. I lost trust. I do not think I even trusted myself. I became an introverted person. I did not figure out who I wanted to be in the future until 2006 and 2007, when I realized that what happened to me in the past should not happen to the next generation to come.

ACU helped me grow spiritually, physically and mentally. It is always important for me to sit down and reflect on my past because when I do that it helps me realize that there is the creator of the world, God, who is the King of kings and owner of everything we see around us. I am convinced that as Christians we should always think about when we will live with God in eternity. As a Christian, I am trying to live my life as if each day were my last day on the earth. This helps me to see every human being as good. I took a test about personality and career goals and I realized I like to spend time with people, persuading people, dialoguing about peace and contributing to the social party. I have a very high emotional interest in others and believe that in leadership I will do a wonderful job according the characteristics of mine I mentioned before.

I have participated in art and sports my whole life. The skills gained in sports and art help, whether I am on the field or working with others in many areas of life. I also like helping others and I like doing the right things. I am developing my interests and strengths, and I am still building and rebuilding myself because even if I am good I still need to be better in terms of making my goals attainable. Even if I am better, I am always working hard to improve whatever I do very well.

I wanted to obtain my masters in Missions and Information Technology (IT) at ACU for so many reasons. ACU is a school where I want to be because of what they have already provided to me as an education. Also, I want to go to a school where I can learn in class and learn spiritually. Then, when I get out of school I can initiate change in people's lives from negative to positive. Like the statement of ACU says: *Educating Christian Leaders for the World*, I see myself leading in the real world by getting my Masters at ACU.

With God everything is possible. As a Christian, being faithful to God can take us far. The past must teach us, but it must not affect us negatively because God is on our side and knows everything about us, even things we do not know about ourselves. I am standing firmly, asking God to fill me with the Spirit; then I can do what is always excellent to Him. My past was bad, but I am convinced that I have a better relationship with our heavenly Father than I ever had. With everything I have I will obey His commands, love others, and glorify God's name.

With my training in psychology, information technology and missions from ACU, I believe it will be beneficial to go back in my country and help. Rwanda is a developing country and those with skills useful to the country rise in leadership positions.

My country is doing a lot of work to get people together again. It is always hard to get people who are not used to getting along to work together. I appreciate what my leaders are doing, and for myself, I am also trying to do the same thing. I believe that most of the trouble my country withstood is due, in large part, to the lack of education. People with higher education are looked to as those with the most significant influence, especially in Rwanda. This is in great part why I am pursuing two master's degrees, because I believe I will have a greater influence. I am convinced that my contribution will help my country. I believe that ACU gave me a firm foundation in my faith and further believe that obtaining my master's degrees from ACU in IT and Missions will only enhance my abilities in Rwanda.

My biggest hope and professional goal is to help others and to protect the rights of the Rwandan people. My people of Rwanda have had so much grief. So much of it was due to lack of education and lack of acceptance. I believe with my education, I can help my country prosper —by leading, by teaching acceptance and love, and by my example.

During the genocide of 1994, everything was destroyed — happiness, security, etc. My long term mission in my country is to contribute to the government's plan of education in technology, theology, leadership and sports. I do believe that God will guide me so that I will obtain these goals. Rwanda has suffered much in the past due to leadership that did not look to the good of all the people in the country. Obtaining a Master of Arts in both Missions and IT, I believe, will provide me with a very strong background that will allow me to communicate well with people of my country who have different mind-sets, beliefs and values.

My greatest desire is to return to Rwanda where I can work with the street children. My goal on my trip back to Rwanda during Christmas 2008 was to see how I could help my country. I found there are great orphanage care opportunities. My wife and I have a dream of providing orphanage care in my home country. It is essential for these young children to have positive role models to look up to and challenge them to be everything God has in store for them to be.

In 2010, I began a foundation to provide medical care for children in Rwanda. I named the foundation Ejo Hazaza – "The Future of Tomorrow." I chose this name because I have a heart for children, and because of the things I saw when I was growing up. When you look at everything that my country, and all the other countries in Africa, went through, you realize that it is our culture that keeps us behind the rest of the world. We lack in education and we do not have a way to provide security for children from infancy through the time they able to take care of themselves. There are some parents out there who just produce children and have no clue how those children will be taken care of, and I see this being a result of the lack of education and a lack of planning knowledge. This is a cultural issue because in the past, people had a lot of land and they gave this land to their children. People might have a lot of cows and the children used the cows to survive without an education. Because people were occupied with caring for the land and the cows, they did not pay attention to education and so they were not aware of what was going on outside of their own comfort zone. Now, all those things are gone and because that culture no longer exists, people are somewhat lost because they have no experience outside their community and so they just live in the past. This lack of education also played a big role in the genocide because it made it easier for the people with education to come in and convince the uneducated people to kill their neighbors who had different beliefs and values. When you are educated, you understand that killing someone with different beliefs will not make you rich or bring you peace.

I look at things from a different perspective now because of living in a different country where children are looked at differently. I realize that children need to be taken care of, so that in the future we have children who are happy, better educated and more emotionally stable. Another reason for wanting to go back is that I knew when I was young some people got sick, and because they had abusive parents or they had no parents, they suffered because no one made sure they saw a doctor and received the medical care they needed. This kept me awake many nights, just thinking how can I sit here in the U.S. and forget where I came from? I thought perhaps I could start something really small, even though I was here and in school. I thought about the idea of being able to get children to hospitals when they are sick. Then I thought that someday I might be able to provide a home for them when they had no one to care for them.

My wife and I had many conversations and even though we were only making minimum wage, which is about $7.25 (U.S.) per hour, we thought we could send $75 a month. At that time, medical care was provided at $2 per child for one year. We started putting our money together and began sending it to the local government to provide medical care. After that, many people became interested and we decided to start a foundation and open it up to other people.

When I started my foundation, I thought that I should not just focus on my family and my relatives, but go outside my tribe to help others because this is how I feel I can bring our people together and one day be one people in the world.

Through my foundation, when I pick out children to pay for their medical care, I pick out children whose parents killed people during the genocide and are now in jail. I pick out children whose parents are from a race other than mine. Because of that, I go to bed feeling good because I feel that I am changing the world from the negative side to a positive side. I hope that one day my dream to unite the whole world will come true. I will work very hard, as I have always worked. I very much desire to be a leader in my country and to live for and show Christ's love to a country so desperately needing love and acceptance.

In 2013, I expanded my Foundation to include a children's home, and changed the name to Rwanda Children. We have been able to build one orphanage already, which houses six children and land has been purchased that will enable us to build more homes. Information about this can be found on our website: www.Rwandachildren.org.

The first children's home built by Rwanda Children, which was founded by Serge Gasore. It was completed in August 2013 and currently houses six children. More information is available at www.Rwandachildren.org.

ABOUT THE AUTHOR

Serge Gasore, Sr. is a native of Rwanda. When he was seven years old, his home land was embroiled in a bitter war known as the Rwandan Genocide. Serge survived the church bombing that killed his grandmother and many other relatives, and managed to stay alive throughout the rest of the genocide by hiding in the bamboo bush, along with many of his fellow Tutsi countrymen. He then served in the Rwandan Patriotic Front until his uncle managed to obtain his discharge and bring him home, where he was able to enroll in school and have the normal life of a child his age. He came to the United States to attend college in August 2005 and enrolled in Abilene Christian University (ACU). In May, 2009 he graduated with a Bachelors in Psychology. He furthered his education with a Master's Degree in Global information Technology Leadership in 2011.

During his undergraduate tenure, Serge received several special awards from ACU. He was presented the Fighting Heart Award, an award given to a student-athlete who advanced themselves both on and off the field without recognition or accolades; the Christian Servant Award, which is given in honor of upholding the principles, philosophy and example of servant-leadership; named to Who's Who Among Students in American Universities & Colleges in 2007 and 2008, an award given in recognition of outstanding merit and accomplishment as a student; and awarded the Dean Adams Achievement Award, which is awarded for recognition for exemplary character, outstanding academic achievement and determined perseverance to overcome obstacles to obtain education.

Serge has served as an ACU Chapel planner, and been invited to present personal lectures by the Associate Dean and Department Chairs. Participation in Spring Board Ideas Challenge adds to his speaking experience. Serge plans to continue implementing his ideas and expanding his network with a PhD in Public Health.

In 2009, Serge partnered with Caleb Beck of Extra Mile Ministry to raise $11,500 specifically for Rwandan orphans and genocide survivors. Other teams Serge has partnered with include World Vision, Team55, and the Texas Department of Aging and Disability Services.

In November of 2010, Serge and his wife, Esperance, established a foundation, Ejo Hazaza, (meaning "The Future of Tomorrow") to provide medical insurance to Rwandan children. They have raised more than $9,000 in support for the children in Rwanda suffering from disease. The foundation provides medical care for more than two thousand Rwandan children. Serge hopes to combine research, lecture opportunities and writing to use his personal story of survival to serve the future generations of Rwanda through medical missions. His goal is to work with the health care organizations in Rwanda to implement sustainable health policies, rebuilding his homeland for future generations.

Serge and Esperance presented a class entitled "Maintaining Hope in Times of Crisis" at the spring 2012 Pepperdine University (Malibu, California) Annual Bible Lectureship.

In 2010, Serge met Dale Dawson, advisor to the President of Rwanda, His Excellence Paul Kagame. He has connected with two other preachers from South Africa, Tebogo Ramatsui and Machona Monyamane, who met to promote their future plans for ministry in Africa.

In the summer of 2013, Serge and Esperance were able to fulfill one of their dreams, when they opened the first children's home in Ntarama, Rwanda, providing housing for four children. They changed the name of their foundation to Rwanda Children and have placed two more children in the home. Other homes will be built and more orphans will find refuge as Rwanda Children continues to grow and provide medical care and housing to the most needy – the children of Rwanda.

Serge and his family currently reside in Abilene,

Texas, where he is currently pursuing a Master's Degree in Global Service at ACU.

Serge Gasore with some of the children who have been placed in the children's home in Ntarama.

CPSIA information can be obtained
at www.ICGtesting.com
Printed in the USA
FSOW01n2044250915
11549FS